RAND PROJECT AIR FORCE

T0288696

Air Force Strategic Planning

Past, Present, and Future

Raphael S. Cohen

Prepared for the United States Air Force

Approved for public release; distribution unlimited

For more information on this publication, visit www.rand.org/t/RR1765

Library of Congress Cataloging-in-Publication Data is available for this publication.

ISBN: 978-0-8330-9697-5

Published by the RAND Corporation, Santa Monica, Calif.

© Copyright 2017 RAND Corporation

RAND® is a registered trademark.

Support RAND

Make a tax-deductible charitable contribution at
www.rand.org/giving/contribute

www.rand.org

Preface

For a relatively young service, the U.S. Air Force has a remarkably rich intellectual history. Even before the Air Force's official formation, the development of airpower has been dotted with such visionaries as Billy Mitchell and Henry "Hap" Arnold. The trend continued after the service's formation with such airmen as John Boyd, Richard "Moody" Suter, and John Warden, who were years, if not decades, ahead of their time. At the same time, however, the Air Force's long-term plans have not always proved particularly farsighted or even notable. Indeed, many of the Air Force's senior leaders are skeptical of long-term strategic planning, and some even question why public strategies are produced altogether.[1]

This study, conducted in RAND Project AIR FORCE's Strategy and Doctrine Program, asks the following question: With the Air Force facing increasing pressure to cut its headquarters staff, are public strategic-planning documents worth the time and energy required to produce them? It looks at what the Air Force has gotten out of its previous strategic-planning efforts. This report examines the evolution of Air Force strategic documents, particularly those produced after the Cold War. The report studies the purpose for these various strategies, the process by which they were created, and the effect these documents had on the service and other key constituencies. It concludes with lessons for Air Force leaders in developing future strategies.

This research was sponsored by the Director of Strategy, Concepts and Assessments, Deputy Chief of Staff for Strategic Plans and Requirements (AF/A5S). It is part of a larger study, titled "Support for USAF Strategic Master Plan Implementation," that assists the Air Force with executing its May 2015 *Strategic Master Plan*.[2]

This report should be of value to the national security community and interested members of the general public, especially those with an interest in strategic plans and the history of the Air Force. Comments are welcome and should be sent to the author, Raphael S. Cohen, or to the project leaders, Michael Mazarr and Sean Zeigler. Research was completed in September 2016.

RAND Project AIR FORCE

RAND Project AIR FORCE (PAF), a division of the RAND Corporation, is the U.S. Air Force's federally funded research and development center for studies and analyses. PAF provides the Air Force with independent analyses of policy alternatives affecting the development, employment, combat readiness, and support of current and future air, space, and cyber forces. Research is

---

[1] Phillip S. Meilinger, "The Problem with Our Air Power Doctrine," *Air Power Journal*, Spring 1992; interview with a retired senior Air Force general officer, January 6, 2016; interview with a retired senior Air Force general officer, April 14, 2016; interview with a retired senior Air Force general officer, September 1, 2016.

[2] U.S. Air Force, *USAF Strategic Master Plan*, May 2015.

conducted in four programs: Force Modernization and Employment; Manpower, Personnel, and Training; Resource Management; and Strategy and Doctrine. The research reported here was prepared under contract FA7014-06-C-0001.

Additional information about PAF is available on our website: www.rand.org/paf/

This report documents work originally shared with the U.S. Air Force on July 18, 2016. The draft report, issued on May 27, 2016, was reviewed by formal peer reviewers and U.S. Air Force subject-matter experts.

Contents

Figure and Tables

Figure

Tables

Summary

For a relatively young service, the U.S. Air Force has a remarkably rich intellectual history. Even before the Air Force's official formation, the development of airpower has been dotted with such visionaries as Billy Mitchell and Henry "Hap" Arnold. The trend continued after the service's formation with such airmen as John Boyd, Richard "Moody" Suter, and John Warden, who were years, if not decades, ahead of their time. At the same time, however, the Air Force's long-term plans have not always proved particularly farsighted or even notable. Indeed, many of the Air Force's senior leaders are skeptical of long-term strategic planning, and some even doubt its utility altogether.[1]

The general dissatisfaction with the state of Air Force strategic planning comes at a time when the Air Force—like its sister services—faces congressional pressure to dramatically reduce its headquarters staff.[2] Given the time and energy required to produce these documents, it raises the question: Is strategic planning worth the effort? After laying out a methodology to answer both questions, this report tells the history of the Air Force's relationship with strategic plans, particularly those produced in the post–Cold War years. It describes how different Air Force leaders have used these strategic plans to define the service's identity, protect the service's budgets on Capitol Hill, carve out new roles and missions, and shape the service's future. More importantly, it accounts for how different Air Force leaders developed, packaged, and sold these documents—with varying degrees of success.

Ultimately, this report argues that, indeed, the Air Force still needs strategic planning but perhaps not in its current form. Throughout its history, the Air Force has successfully used strategic planning to accomplish four basic tasks: allocate and justify resources; structure the force; define and shape the service's mission and even identity; and, perhaps most importantly, create a dialogue about the direction of the service. Arguably, five major lessons have made certain strategies comparatively successful—namely, the importance of encouraging ideas from the bottom; knowing and aligning with the policy environment; developing and pushing strategy from the top; clearly articulating the service's needs; and understanding that, in the end, the process is sometimes more important than the final product. Understanding these five basic lessons may not guarantee that the Air Force can produce truly innovative institutional strategy, but it may allow it to make the most out of the process.

---

[1] Phillip S. Meilinger, "The Problem with Our Air Power Doctrine," *Air Power Journal*, Spring 1992; interview with a retired senior Air Force general officer, January 6, 2016; interview with a retired senior Air Force general officer, April 14, 2016; interview with a retired senior Air Force general officer, September 1, 2016.

[2] Charles Clark, "Pentagon Orders Even More HQ Cuts, Infuriating Employees' Union," *Defense One*, September 9, 2015.

Acknowledgments

I would like to thank Michael J. Mazarr and Sean Zeigler for their guidance and thoughtful critiques of earlier drafts of this report. Paula Thornhill, Alan Vick, Dick Anderegg, former Secretary of the U.S. Air Force Donald Rice, Richard Darilek, and Maj Gen (ret.) Michael Snodgrass also offered helpful suggestions for this report. Patrick Harding of the Air Force A5 and Clark Murdock, formerly of the Center for Strategic and International Studies and the Air Staff, helped with the research phase, filling the intellectual gaps and providing primary sources. I also want to thank Brenna Allen, Rebeca Orrie, and Sean Zeigler for assisting with the interviews for this project. Linda Theung also provided expert editorial assistance. Perhaps most importantly, I would like to thank the dozen and a half Air Force senior civilian and military leaders who consented to be interviewed for this report. Because of human-subjects protection protocols, I cannot thank them by name; their insights proved invaluable in understanding how Air Force strategic planning has evolved over the decades.

Abbreviations

AFM	Air Force Manual
AWPD	Air War Plans Division
CONUS	continental United States
CSAF	Chief of Staff of the U.S Air Force
DoD	U.S. Department of Defense
EAGLE	Evolutionary Air and Space Global Laser Engagement
FM	field manual
FY	fiscal year
ISR	intelligence, surveillance, and reconnaissance
QDR	Quadrennial Defense Review
TAC	Tactical Air Command
UAV	unmanned aerial vehicles

1. Strategic Planning and Its Discontents

Former Chief of Staff of the U.S. Air Force (CSAF) Gen Michael Dugan worried, "We're a service of technology as opposed to strategy."[1] Dugan's fears echo several other senior leaders' frustration with Air Force strategic planning. Despite a rich intellectual tradition, the Air Force has not always embraced strategic planning as an institution, and some of its senior leaders have questioned the purposes for these documents altogether. When asked why he chose to write a strategic plan despite doubting the plan's effect, a former Air Force senior general officer replied, "Well, it's kind of like why you decorate your house for Christmas. Sometimes, it's just far too painful not to."[2] In response to a similar question, another former senior Air Force general officer quipped, "In the Air Force you have a bunch of lieutenant colonels sitting around with nothing else to do except write papers." He added, "you can't be against long range planning; it's like who's going to be against apple pie?"[3] A third retired senior Air Force general officer lamented that, while earlier Air Force strategies served a purpose, today's documents are "full of fluff and gobbledygook."[4] A fourth former senior Air Force general officer echoed this critique and argued that "we [the Air Force] are stuck in talking about airpower in grand terms and not war-fighting in grand terms."[5]

Observers have offered a host of explanations for the Air Force's attitudes toward long-range planning encounters. In his study of Air Force strategic planning, Colin Campbell suggests that the Air Force struggles with strategic planning because of its size and complexity. Campbell notes that the Air Force represented about 4 percent of the U.S. federal budget—or, in absolute terms, only $21 billion less—than the entire Australian government's budget in fiscal year (FY) 2000.[6] Air Force officer and scholar Phillip Meilinger argues that the Air Force's planning woes stem from the way pilots are trained: "Becoming proficient in an F-15 or F-16 could easily dominate an aviator's life, and little time remained to consider anything other than the tactical aspects of air war."[7] Retired Gen Charles Boyd gives a more tongue-in-cheek explanation:

---

[1] Interview with a retired senior Air Force general officer quoting General Dugan, May 11, 2016; for similar sentiments, see Phillip S. Meilinger, "The Problem with Our Air Power Doctrine," *Air Power Journal*, Spring 1992. Another former Air Force senior leader recounted Dugan, expressing similar sentiments (interview with an Air Force senior civilian leader, September 16, 2016).

[2] Interview with a retired senior Air Force general officer, January 6, 2016.

[3] Interview with a retired senior Air Force general officer, April 14, 2016.

[4] Interview with a retired senior Air Force general officer, September 1, 2016

[5] Interview with a retired senior Air Force general officer, October 11, 2016

[6] Colin Campbell, "Long-Range Corporate Strategic Planning in Government Organizations: The Case of the U.S. Air Force," *Governance*, Vol. 15, No. 4, October 2002, p. 429.

[7] Meilinger, 1992

"Flying is so much sheer fun that no normal fighter pilot would want to consider something more abstract."[8] Others suggest that Air Force strategy—like military strategy more broadly—simply struggles to keep pace with a rapidly changing world. The former commander of Strategic Air Command and U.S. Strategic Command Gen George Lee Butler analogized, "In many respects, the recasting of military strategy has been very much like painting the proverbial moving train— the cars are familiar, but they refuse to stand still as powerful new forces fuel the boiler of the strategic locomotive."[9]

Whatever the reason, the general dissatisfaction with the state of Air Force strategic planning comes at a time when the Air Force—like its sister services—faces congressional pressure to dramatically reduce its headquarters staff.[10] Given the time and effort required to produced these documents, it raises the question: Is strategic planning worth the effort? This study attempts to answer this question in five sections. First, it briefly lays out a methodology for studying the effect of strategy on a military service. Second, it reviews the evolution of Air Force strategy from its beginnings through the end of the Cold War and argues that, while many of the most influential documents came from far-sighted visionaries operating outside of formal channels, official documents proved critical in a different respect—carving out the Air Force's role as an independent service. The third section, the empirical heart of this study, analyzes the major Air Force strategies since the end of the Cold War and details how different service secretaries and chiefs of staff approached long-range planning differently. Fourth, it offers five major lessons for what made certain strategies successful. Finally, in a short postscript, it offers thoughts about the future of Air Force strategy in a resource-constrained age. Ultimately, this study argues that, if done well, strategic planning can accomplish four basic tasks: Allocate and justify resources; structure the force; define and shape the service's mission and even identity; and, perhaps most importantly, create a dialogue about the direction of the service. Doing strategic planning "well," in turn, requires applying five basic lessons: understanding the policy environment; encouraging ideas from the bottom; starting the strategy from the top; keeping the message succinct, substantive, and sharp; and focusing on process as much as product.

---

[8] Quoted in Meilinger, 1992.

[9] George L. Butler, "Adjusting to Post–Cold War Strategic Realities," *Parameters*, Spring 1991, p. 9.

[10] Charles Clark, "Pentagon Orders Even More HQ Cuts, Infuriating Employees' Union," *Defense One*, September 9, 2015.

2. Defining Strategy and Measuring Its Effect

Before evaluating an organization's use of strategy, we must first determine the proper unit of analysis. Simply put, what counts as a strategy? The answer is less clear than it might seem. As a service, the Air Force is not legally required to produce a strategy, and for most of its history, there was no single, definitive "Air Force strategy." In theory, strategy should include ends (what are the ultimate objectives), ways (how to get there), and means (what resources it will employ to accomplish these goals) for the entire service. In practice, however, the Air Force only rarely attempted to combine all three elements into a single comprehensive, servicewide, publicly released strategy. Instead, it often chose to divide ends, ways, and means between different documents. Consequently, there is no set canon of "Air Force strategies"; rather, there is a loose collection of Air Force "strategic documents" that vary by context and period.

Through the end of the Cold War, Air Force strategies took a more amorphous, if ad hoc, shape than they do today. Most directly, war plans guided the use, size, and stationing of the force. Senior airpower leaders also offered occasional statements that charted out how they saw the future for airpower. Periodically, the Air Force staff also issued special reports detailing how future technology might affect the service and how new concepts might be implemented. Later, they issued "road maps" detailing what types of platforms the service intended to buy. Although these documents often had a more programmatic and technological edge, they had as much—if not more—say in shaping the future of service than more traditional strategy documents. By determining what types of capabilities the Air Force would invest in, these documents *de facto* determined how the Air Force would structure itself and fight future conflicts.

Doctrine—although not commonly viewed today as a "strategy," since it details how the service operates today rather than how it should operate in the future—also played an important role in the early years, as the Army Air Corps struggled to define its roles and missions and assert its independence. Given the emphasis that the Army places on doctrine, codifying airpower's role in these formal documents became one of the best ways to guarantee its independence in the future. Later, during the Cold War, the Air Force still used doctrine—specifically Air Force Manual (AFM) 1-2, *United States Air Force Basic Doctrine*—to define its mission and purpose. Only in the post–Cold War period, when *Global Reach—Global Power* was published,[1] did the Air Force attempt to codify its purpose in a stand-alone strategic document.

The publication of *Global Reach—Global Power* proved a watershed event for Air Force strategic planning. For the first time, the senior service leadership issued a stand-alone document

---

[1] Donald B. Rice, *The Air Force and U.S. National Security: Global Reach—Global Power*, white paper, Washington, D.C.: Department of the Air Force, June 1990a.

attempting to define "just how the U.S. Air Force contributed to national security."[2] While previous Air Force leaders had penned articles, given speeches, or issued guidance, *Global Reach—Global Power* was different in that it was official and included a significant public rollout in ways that other strategies had not. Its publication prompted a series of other vision documents by succeeding Secretaries of the Air Force and Chiefs of Staff.

Over the next quarter century, Air Force strategy became both more public and more formalized—with a series of types of products produced on a semiregular basis (see Figure 2.1). Drawing on national and U.S. Department of Defense (DoD) strategy, today's Air Force produces service-vision documents outlining in broad terms what the Air Force does and where it wants to go; operating concepts detailing how it plans to fight; road maps charting what it wants to buy; strategic plans for what policies and procedures it wants to implement; and doctrine, although the importance of doctrine relative to the other strategic documents has diminished.

Figure 2.1. Today's Strategic Documents

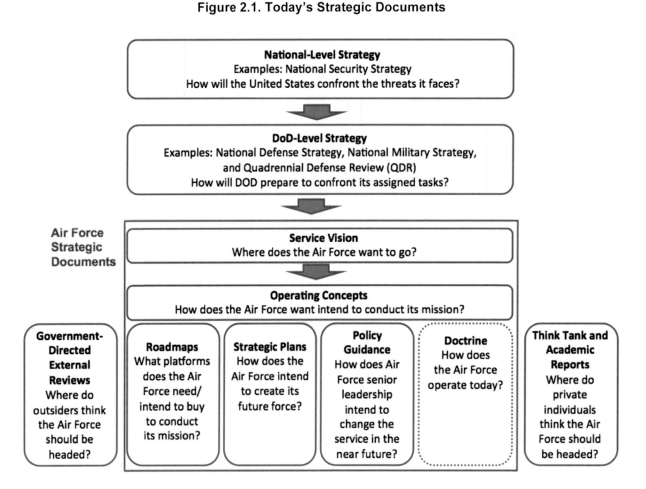

---

[2] Richard P. Hallion, *Storm over Iraq: Air Power and the Gulf War*, Washington, D.C.: Smithsonian Institution Press, 1992, p. 119.

Air Force strategy documents, however, differ from national- and defense-level strategies in at least two important ways. First, unlike such national-level policy documents as the *National Security Strategy* or DoD-level documents (e.g., the *National Defense Strategy* or the *Quadrennial Defense Review* [QDR]), the Air Force—like the other services—are not legally required to produce a "strategy." As a result, what specific documents are produced vary depending on the Chief of Staff and the Service Secretary at the time. Second, service-level documents often need to look at a longer time horizon than many national- and defense-level documents, particularly because the time required to develop and field new capabilities to the force can take a decade or longer, which is beyond the lifetime of any administration. Indeed, these different time horizons can create friction between investing in the needs of the future versus managing problems of today.

Ultimately, this report mostly focuses on Air Force strategic documents (outlined in the red box in Figure 2.1), with a particular emphasis on post–Cold War developments, when Air Force strategy really began to take shape. Chapter Three, which covers the Air Force's origins through the Cold War period, focuses on a somewhat different set of documents and places emphasis on doctrine (based largely on the latter's significance during the early years of the service). For the most part, the report does not address outside organizations' strategies (i.e., those produced by think tanks, academic, or even government-sponsored reviews), since the focus here is on Air Force strategic planning, not strategic planning about the Air Force.

A few caveats about scope, however, are in order. First, this report focuses on institutional rather than warfighting strategies or, more specifically, how the Air Force generates and maintains forces rather than how it fights individual wars (which now is the purview of the combatant commands rather than Air Force headquarters). Second, the study looks only at strategic documents designed to shape the Air Force comprehensively, rather than specific policies. For example, the Air Force publishes strategies for specific technological areas (e.g., remote-piloted aircraft) or personnel (e.g., diversity within the force), but for reasons of space, this work limits itself to comprehensive documents affecting multiple facets of the service. Third, also for reasons of space, this report does not offer a comprehensive, year-by-year history of Air Force budgeting or the Program Objective Memorandums, the regularly produced planning documents that shape it, or the statements by the service secretaries and CSAFs to U.S. Congress to justify it. It does, however, look at larger, more ad hoc documents, some of which ultimately profoundly shaped the Air Force and the Program Objective Memorandum.

If defining what constitutes a "strategy" is difficult, then defining what it means to do strategy "well" proves even more ambiguous. Strategies differ in scope and ambitions, complicating cross-case comparisons. Moreover, many strategies' true objectives are not always clear. Often unclassified, publicly released strategies do not clearly spell out concrete changes, leaving analysts to decipher the true motivations for the document by reading between the lines. Even if the motives are known, not all strategies are alike in desired scope and effect. Some have grand objectives and aim to reshape the service for decades to come. Others are more tactical in nature, designed as signals to specific constituencies and a way to influence certain policy debates. As such, before exploring the strategies themselves, we first need to develop a common set of benchmarks to guide an evaluation.[3]

One obvious criterion to apply to judge the effect of any public strategy is whether it gets read and, if so, by whom? All publicly released strategies presumably hope to attract readers, although which audience is deemed most important often varies. Some aim at servicemembers themselves.[4] Others try to speak to Congress and policymakers who control the purse strings. Still others want to influence an even wider audience—think tanks, academics, and even international audiences—to help shape the broader policy sphere. These public documents can even serve a foreign policy goal, signaling support to allies of the United States and deterring its adversaries.[5] No matter the intended audience, however, the most basic metric of success is whether the intended audience takes notice. There are several ways to evaluate this measure of impression: How often a document is downloaded, whether it generates press coverage, how often it is cited in scholarship, and how adversaries react are all indirect measures of readership.

A second measure of effect is whether a strategy leads to shifts in resources—that is, in how the Air Force spends its budget or dedicates its manpower. Importantly, this does not equate to a strategy's effectiveness. The raw numbers tell little about whether a strategy was, in retrospect, a "good" idea, but they do provide a quantifiable measure of change produced—for better or worse—by the service.

A third measure is permanence. As we will see, many Air Force senior leaders developed their own vision for the service that they articulated during their tenure and infused it—to varying extents—into official documents. One senior Air Force officer remarked, "Everybody wants their DNA to survive . . . to ensure their place in the gene pool. That's why they do and redo these kinds of long-range planning efforts and documents."[6] What separates these visions is how well they stand the test of time and outlast their original authors.

Importantly, we should be explicit about what is *not* used as an evaluation criterion here—namely, whether the strategy was "right" or "wrong." Each strategy is a product of a unique set of historical circumstances, some more complex than others. Passing judgment on the strategy requires fully understanding these circumstances, evaluating alternative courses of action, and playing out the counterfactual (i.e., what would have happened if the Air Force pursued another approach). In other words, judgments on strategy would require a far more analytically demanding task than what was set out as the scope of this study. Instead, in an admittedly more

---

[3] For a similar attempt to assess the effect of doctrine, see Raphael S. Cohen, "A Tale of Two Manuals," *Prism*, Vol. 2, No. 1, December 2011.

[4] Interview with a former Air Force senior leader, April 21, 2016.

[5] Interview with a retired senior Air Force general officer, January 6, 2016.

[6] Interview with a retired senior Air Force general officer, April 14, 2016.

modest and imperfect approach, our analysis focuses more on the process surrounding the development and implementation and why some were well received while others fell flat.

Finally, we should touch on the sources used in this analysis. First and foremost, this study analyzes the strategic documents themselves to try and understand their aims. It then examines scholarly and journalistic accounts to better understand the processes behind these documents' creations, these documents' effect on the service, and their reception both within and beyond the Air Force. Finally, this study also draws on more than 15 interviews with senior leaders— principally, the heads of the strategic-planning efforts on the Air Force staff, the CSAFs, and the service secretaries—from a range of historical periods to understand the story behind these strategies from the perspectives of those who wrote them and from the senior leaders who provided the vision and implemented them.

There are, however, two limitations with the data. First, since this is an unclassified study, it did not examine any of the classified versions of these plans or classified correspondence surrounding their creation. Second, it also did not look at the archival material, largely because much of the archives for more-recent plans remain classified. As a result, this report is admittedly incomplete. And, with these caveats in mind, we can turn to the history of Air Force strategic thinking.

3. Air Force Strategy from Its Formation Through the Cold War

Even before the Air Force became a separate and equal service, it developed a reputation for innovative thinking. Starting in the aftermath of World War I, American Billy Mitchell and such fellow pioneers as Italian Giulio Douhet, Briton Sir Hugh Trenchard, and Russian pilot and American airpower strategist Alexander de Seversky foresaw the potential of airpower and were vocal advocates within their respective militaries about its potential. These strategists' effect long outlived their own tenures in the service. Indeed, Douhet's classic book *Command of the Air* remains on the Air Force's Air University's website today.[1] Importantly, these early airpower advocates often developed their ideas, publications, followings, and influence outside of—and sometimes in opposition to—their own military bureaucracies. Even when these militaries produced official airpower strategies, they were often less innovative and arguably less influential than these visionaries' writings. Nonetheless, early Army Air Corps and later Air Force strategic documents still served three primary functions: They allocated and justified resources; structured the force; and, perhaps most importantly of all, helped define the Air Force's purpose and mission. Ultimately, these early decades teach an important lesson about these documents' utility: Written by committees under careful supervision from layers of bureaucracy, official strategies are—by design—unlikely to be revolutionary documents, but they can still play a crucial role at defining the status quo, carving out bureaucratic turf, and cementing institutional culture.

The Army Air Corps/Army Air Force

Although airpower advocates were often outspoken and bold in their development of strategic concepts, the official Army Air Corps' documents proved far more timid. Even the medium for expressing the Air Corps' strategic concepts had a fundamentally conservative bias. Before becoming an independent service, the most-important official statements about the roles and missions of the Air Corps came not in strategy but in doctrine, and doctrine, unlike strategy, does not focus on how the Army should fight within its present capabilities. Given this, rather than envisioning what airpower *could* accomplish in the future, Army doctrine detailed how airpower functioned in today's fight.

Perhaps unsurprisingly, the initial attempts at Air Corps doctrine argued in favor of a limited role for airpower. For example, on January 26, 1926, the Air Corps published Training

---

[1] Giulio Douhet, *Command of the Air*, trans. Dino Ferrari, Washington, D.C.: Air Force History and Museums Program, 1998.

Regulation 440-15, *Fundamental Principles for the Employment of the Air Service*.[2] Revised in 1935 and later in 1940, the training regulation became the founding doctrinal document of the Air Corps. Unlike the early airpower advocates who saw airpower at the center of the future combat, the Training Regulation envisioned the Air Corps principally performing a fairly modest role—providing close air support to ground forces.[3] Ultimately, these early debates about doctrine in the 1920s and 1930s were more than just a debate about obscure training manuals; they were debates about bureaucratic identity and doctrine that became the vehicle for defining turf. As Air Force analyst Benjamin Lambeth argues, they were attempts to "earn a place at the table for airpower in the development of national military strategy and capability."[4]

Even in the run-up to World War II, doctrine continued to officially curtail the role of airpower as independent actor. On April 15, 1940, under the direction of then–Lt Col (later CSAF) Gen Carl Spaatz, the Army Air Corps published its first official doctrine—Field Manual (FM) 1-5, *Employment of the Aviation of the Army*.[5] Unfortunately, for political reasons, "the Air Corps' unwritten doctrine and commitment to strategic attack was, for all intents and purposes, not even mentioned. It is apparent from this that the War Department was still in control of Air Corps doctrine and producing material in which the airmen had little or no faith."[6]

Army Air Force strategic planning for World War II deserves credit for pushing for a larger independent role for the nascent service. Given the limited role prescribed to airpower in such official doctrine as Training Regulation 440-15, many in the Army Air Corps feared that, left to their own devices, ground-centric Army planners would relegate airpower to a subordinate role.[7] Given this, when Germany invaded Russia in summer 1941, then–head of the Army Air Corps Henry "Hap" Arnold insisted that his staff write the plan for how airpower should be used to defeat U.S. "potential enemies" rather than leave the planning to the Army at large. The plan—ultimately labeled Air War Plans Division 1 (AWPD-1)—called for a six-month strategic air campaign before the actual invasion of Germany and laid out the forces it believed it needed to accomplish this aim.[8] About a year later, on August 25, 1942, at the request of President Franklin

---

[2] War Department Training Regulations, *Air Service: Fundamental Principles for the Employment of the Air Service*, Washington, D.C., TR 440-15, January 26, 1926.

[3] James A. Mowbray, "Air Force Doctrine Problems: 1926–Present," *Air and Space Power Journal*, Winter 1995, p. 2.

[4] Benjamin S. Lambeth, *The Transformation of American Air Power*, Ithaca, N.Y.: Cornell University Press, 2000, p. 258.

[5] U.S. Government Printing Office, *Army Air Forces Field Manual: Employment of Aviation of the Army*, Washington, D.C., FM 1-5, 1943.

[6] Mowbray, 1995, p. 5.

[7] Haywood S. Hansell, Jr., *The Air Plan That Defeated Hitler*, Atlanta, Ga.: Higgins-McArthur/Longino and Porter, Inc., 1972, p. 64.

[8] Hansell, 1972, p. 78.

D. Roosevelt, the Air Staff updated the estimate of its future needs in another plan, AWPD-42.[9] This revised plan, however, shared many of the same basic strategic assumptions of AWPD-1, including a strategic offensive in Europe.[10]

AWPD-1 and AWPD-42 were not, at least in the traditional sense, service strategies (they were more a combination of a war plan and air doctrine), but they still played an important role in developing the Army Air Force as an institution in two respects. First, they outlined how the Army Air Force should spend its resources. AWPD-1 called for 2,164,916 officers and men, manning some 251 combat groups, with a total fleet of 61,799 aircraft.[11] AWPD-42 called for a somewhat larger force of 2,734,347 officers and enlisted, 281 combat groups, and some 127,000 airplanes—85,300 of which would go to the Army Air Force.[12] Ultimately, these estimates proved largely accurate; the actual figures for manpower were off the AWPD-1 numbers by 5.5 percent and combat groups were off by only 2 percent.[13] Second and as important, AWPD-1 and AWPD-42 helped secure the Air Force's role as independent entity. Air Force Maj Gen Haywood Hansell argued that the "moment of conception of the United States Air Force" was when AWPD-1 was briefed to Army Chief of Staff GEN George Marshall, and he accepted its premises.[14] By agreeing to such a massive build-up of the Army Air Force and a strategic air campaign against Germany, Marshall helped pave the way for Army Air Force as an institution.

The development of FM 100-20, *Command and Employment of Air Power*, published on July 21, 1943, further helped define the Army Air Force's mission and future.[15] Although originally only 14 pages long, the doctrine had an outsized effect.[16] It prioritized tactical air missions—air superiority, interdiction, and close support.[17] Beyond that, though, it made an important political statement. According to the late Air University Professor James Mowbray, the doctrine's "most notable feature" came in its first line.[18] It proclaimed: "land power and air

[9] Hansell, 1972, p. 100.

[10] Hansell, 1972, p. 102; and Haywood S. Hansell, Jr., *The Strategic Air Plan Against Germany and Japan: A Memoir*, Washington, D.C.: Office of Air Force History, United States Air Force, 1986, pp. 58–59.

[11] Hansell, 1972, p. 88; and Hansell, 1986, p. 37. Notably, this figure did not include the number of replacement aircraft to replace attrition. This figure was placed at about 59,400 (Hansell, 1986, p. 39).

[12] The rest would go to the U.S. Navy; see Hansell, 1972, p. 109; and Hansell, 1986, p. 60.

[13] Hansell, 1972, p. 193.

[14] Hansell, 1986, p. 40.

[15] Mowbray, 1995, p. 5.

[16] War Department Field Manual, *Command and Employment of Air Power*, Washington, D.C.: U.S. Government Printing Office, FM 100-20, July 21, 1943.

[17] Mowbray, 1995, p. 5.

[18] Mowbray, 1995, p. 5.

power are co-equal and interdependent forces; neither is an auxiliary of the other."[19] Given the Army's emphasis on doctrine, this statement had outsized importance in asserting the Army Air Force's growing independence as institution. Indeed, some even label FM 100-20 as the "Air Force's Declaration of Independence."[20]

Yet a third example of the interplay between strategic planning and protecting bureaucratic identity comes from Air Staff's Special Projects office and, perhaps more importantly, the Post War Division of the Air Staff.[21] According to some accounts, the offices were created largely for "parochial reasons"—to push for greater autonomy for the Air Force.[22] And, despite being in existence since 1943, the Post War Division managed to avoid being sucked into planning the war and focused on what happened next for the nascent service.[23] In February 1944, the Post War Division produced *Initial Postwar Air Force: Preliminary Study by Assistant Chief of the Air Force Staff, Plans*, which called for 105 groups and 1 million airmen to active duty.[24] Beyond the topline numbers, the Post War Division also began to work out other issues—such as where the Air Force would be based.[25] Ultimately, the Post War Division work received mixed reviews. The Air Force ultimately adopted a force that was significantly smaller than what was initially proposed (some 70 groups), and Air Force historian and Maj Gen Perry Smith wrote, "It [the Post War Division] opened no new policy vistas, did no really creative planning, and it formed assumptions to justify force levels in a very limited sense."[26] Still, it did help accomplish its larger mission: pushing for a large, independent service.

Perhaps a more important Air Force strategy was General Arnold's "Air Power and the Future: Third Report to the Secretary of War by the Commanding General of the Army Air Forces," dated November 12, 1945. Described by some scholars as a "visionary" document, it outlined the roles and mission for the Army Air Forces at the conclusion of World War II.[27] The document reviewed the war's lessons for airpower and included sections on training, intelligence, and research and development.[28] More importantly, "Air Power and the Future"

---

[19] War Department Field Manual, 1943, p. 1; see, also, Perry McCoy Smith, *The Air Force Plans for Peace, 1943–1945*, Baltimore, Md.: Johns Hopkins Press, 1970, p. 21.

[20] Hallion, 1992, p. 13.

[21] Smith, 1970, p. 5.

[22] Smith, 1970, p. 107.

[23] Smith, 1970, p. 13.

[24] Smith, 1970, p. 57.

[25] Smith, 1970, pp. 75–83.

[26] Smith, 1970, p. 115.

[27] Peter Hays and Karl Mueller, "Going Boldly—Where? Aerospace Integration, the Space Commission, and the Air Force's Vision for Space," *Aerospace Power Journal*, Spring 2001, p. 36.

[28] Henry H. Arnold, "Air Power and the Future," in Eugene M. Emme, ed., *The Impact of Air Power: National Security and World Politics*, Princeton, N.J.: D. Van Nostrand Company, Inc., 1959.

served as a political statement. It declared that "Air Power will always be the business of every American citizen." Furthermore, it predicted

> [i]n any future war the Air Force, being unique among the armed services in its ability to reach any possible enemy without long delay, will undoubtedly be the first to engage the enemy and, if this is done early enough, it may remove the necessity for extended surface conflict.[29]

Ultimately, Arnold's comments reflected his beliefs about the lessons learned from World War II: The combination of nuclear weapons, long-range bombers, and ballistic missiles secured the Air Force's leading role in future conflicts and a brewing turf battle with the Navy over power projection and the nuclear mission.[30]

Arnold also commissioned the multivolume *Toward New Horizons*,[31] another, perhaps equally important if more scientific, document. As a mark of strategic planning, the study was the "first exhaustive review of science as it related to the military services."[32] Led by Arnold's scientific adviser, the Hungarian-Jewish scientist Theodore von Kármán, the study looked at the implications of scientific advances for airpower. Beginning work in fall 1944 and concluding late the following year, Von Kármán successfully predicted key trends that would later define airpower, including supersonic flight, target-seeking missiles, missiles able to reach thousands of

---

[29] Barbara J. Faulkenberry, *Global Reach—Global Power: Air Force Strategic Vision, Past and Future*, Maxwell Air Force Base, Ala.: Air University Press, 1996, pp. 14–15.

[30] Hallion, 1992, pp. 14–15.

[31] See Theodore Von Karman, *Toward New Horizons*, Vol. 1., Cameron Station, Alexandria, Va.: Defense Documentation Center for Scientific and Technical Information, 1945; Theodore Von Karman, *Where We Stand: A Report Prepared for the AAF Scientific Advisory Group*, Vol. 2, Dayton, Ohio: Wright Field, May 1946; H. S. Tsien, H. L. Dryden, F. L. Wattendorf, F. W. Williams, F. Zwicky, and W. H. Pickering, *Technical Intelligence Supplement: A Report to the AAF Scientific Advisory Group*, Vol. 3, Dayton, Ohio: Wright Field, May 1946; H. S. Hsien, W. R. Sears, Iriving L. Ashkenas, C. N. Hasert, and N. M. Newmark, *Aerodynamics and Aircraft Design: A Report of the AAF Scientific Advisory* Group, Vol. 4, Dayton, Ohio: Wright Field, May 1946; T. F. Walkowicz, *Toward New Horizons*, Vol. 5, *Future Airborne Armies*, Dayton, Ohio: Wright Field, September 1945; Frank L. Wattendorf, H. S. Hsien, and Pol Duwez, *Aircraft Power Plants: A Report to the AAF Scientific Advisory Group*, Vol. 6, Dayton, Ohio: Wright Field, May 1946; W. J. Sweeney, L. P. Hammett, A. J. Stosick, and H. S. Tsien, *Aircraft Fuels and Propellants: A Report Prepared for the AAF Scientific Advisory Group*, Vol. 7, Dayton, Ohio: Wright Field, May 1946; H. L. Dryden, W. H. Pickering, H. S. Tsien, and G. B. Schubauer, *Guided Missiles and Pilotless Aircraft: A Report Prepared for the AAF Scientific Advisory Group*, Vol. 8, Dayton, Ohio: Wright Field, May 1946; H. L. Dryden, G. A. Morton, I. A. Getting, *Guidance and Homing of Missiles and Pilotless Aircraft: A Report for the AAF Scientific Advisory Group*, Vol. 9, Dayton, Ohio: Wright Field, May 1946; D. P. Mac Dougall and N. M. Newmark, *Explosives and Terminal Ballistics: A Report Prepared for the AAF Scientific Advisory Group*, Vol. 10, Dayton, Ohio: Wright Field, May 1946; L. A. Dubridge, E. M. Purcell, G. A. Morton, and G. E. Valley, *Radar and Communications: A Report Prepared for the AAF Scientific Advisory Group*, Vol. 11, Dayton, Ohio: Wright Field, May 1946; Irving P. Krick, *War and Weather: A Report Prepared for the AAF Scientific Advisory Group*, Dayton, Ohio: Wright Field, May 1946; and W. R. Lovelace, A. P. Gagge, and C. W. Bray, *Aviation Medicine and Psychology: A Report Prepared for the AAF Scientific Advisory Group*, Dayton, Ohio: Wright Field, May 1946.

[32] Michael H. Gorn, ed., *Prophecy Fulfilled: "Toward New Horizons" and Its Legacy*, Washington, D.C.: Air Force History and Museums Program, 1994, p. 16.

miles, and all-weather navigation systems.[33] Widely praised by the Army Air Force leadership at the time, *Toward New Horizons* had multilayered legacy. Most immediately, it helped guide Air Force research and development efforts over the next several decades.[34] More broadly, it paved the way for future large-scale scientific reviews by the Air Force that would shape its approach to long-term strategic planning in the decades to come.

While "Air Power and the Future" laid out the Air Force's future and *Toward New Horizons* outlined the future of Air Force science behind airpower, *Survival in the Air Age: A Report by the President's Air Policy Commission* charted a course for all American aviation. On July 18, 1947, President Harry S. Truman appointed lawyer-turned-statesman and future Secretary of the Air Force Thomas K. Finletter to review U.S. aviation policies.[35] The wide-ranging review published on January 1, 1948, months after the Air Force's founding, proclaimed,

> In our opinion this Military Establishment must be built around the air arm. Of course an adequate Navy and Ground Force must be maintained. But it is the Air Force and naval aviation on which we must mainly rely. Our military security must be based on air power.[36]

Survival in the Air Age predicted a world with multiple nuclear actors, where the U.S. homeland would be—for the first time in its history—under direct threat from foreign adversaries.[37] As a result, the Air Force itself needed to be "strong, well equipped and modern, not only capable of meeting the attack when it comes but, even more important, capable of dealing a crushing counteroffensive blow on the aggressor."[38]

Importantly, *Survival in the Air Age* was a U.S. government, rather than an Air Force, document, and, as such, it differed in scope and substance from later Air Force service–specific strategies. Arguably, its vision of a military with the Air Force at its core was never fully realized. Still, by the three measures set forth in Chapter Two, *Survival in the Air Age* proved a success. It attracted a national-level audience. It helped secured the Air Force's resources—commanding roughly one-third of all defense in FY 1948, eventually rising to almost one-half of all defense spending a decade later.[39] Finally, it assisted in slowly carving out and institutionalizing the Air Force's role as an independent and coequal service.

---

[33] Gorn, 1994, p. 9.

[34] Gorn, 1944, p. 15.

[35] Robert Frank Futrell, *Ideas, Concepts, Doctrine: Basic Thinking in the United States Air Force, 1907–1960*, Vol. 1, Maxwell Air Force Base, Ala.: Air University Press, December 1989a, p. 225.

[36] President's Air Policy Commission, *Survival in the Air Age: A Report by the President's Air Policy Commission*, Washington D.C.: U.S. Government Printing Office, January 1, 1948, p. 8.

[37] President's Air Policy Commission, 1948, p. 13.

[38] President's Air Policy Commission, 1948, pp. 11–12.

[39] Kevin N. Lewis, *The U.S. Air Force Budget and Posture over Time*, Santa Monica, Calif.: RAND Corporation, R-3807-AF, 1990, p. 12.

From the Air Force's Founding Until the Vietnam War

In its early years, Air Force senior leaders often publicized their vision for the future of the service in a variety of venues. Congressional testimony provided one avenue, particularly for procurement priorities. Air Force senior leaders sometimes penned articles in professional journals, such as *Air Force Magazine.* Although the Air Force did not issue separate vision documents in the same way as it did in the post–Cold War period, Air Force doctrine indirectly hinted at the service's vision, particularly the AFM 1-2, *United States Air Force Basic Doctrine.* The first version of the *Basic Doctrine* was published on April 1, 1953, and was motivated by the fact that "airpower had not done very well in Korea *in light of what it promised and could not deliver.*"[40] In particular, the doctrine attempted to think through the perceived failure of the strategic bombing effort during the Korean War.[41] Arguably, this reconsideration did not last long or go very deep. Fighter pilots may have seen the world differently, but the Air Force's leadership—controlled primarily by bomber pilots who cut their intellectual teeth during World War II—saw the Air Force's principle missions as strategic bombing and waging nuclear war even after the former's lack of success in the Korean War. Indeed, the greatest of these officers, Gen LeMay, who became CSAF in 1961, later remarked, "I think we have been consistent in our concepts since the formation of the GHQ [general headquarters] Air Force in 1935. Our basic doctrine has remained generally unchanged since that time."[42]

Still, early versions of the *Basic Doctrine* did make some key changes to the vision for the future role of the service. The April 25, 1958, version used the term "aerospace power," since the Air Force now had "moved naturally and inevitably to higher altitudes and higher speeds until it now stands on the threshold of space operation."[43] The then-CSAF Thomas D. White coined the term to capture his vision for the future of airpower—as seamlessly extending from air into space, a concept that the Air Force has wrestled with ever since.[44] In a sense, these doctrinal debates were more than questions of terminology or proper operating procedure: They were attempts to define the role and identity of the service itself.

Aside from Air Force doctrine, perhaps the most common way for the Air Force's senior leadership to disseminate their vision was through the "Information Policy Letters for

---

[40] Mowbray, 1995, p. 6 (emphasis in the original); also see, Futrell, 1989a, p. 393.

[41] Mowbray, 1995, p. 6. Strategic bombing argued that one could defeat an adversary by destroying its industrial base. During the Korean War, however, much of North Korea's warmaking potential was located in China and the Soviet Union, both politically off limits to Air Force bombing efforts (Jeffery J. Smith, *Tomorrow's Air Force: Tracing the Past, Shaping the Future,* Bloomington, Ind.: Indiana University Press, 2013, p. 63).

[42] Michael Worden, *Rise of the Fighter Generals. The Problem of Air Force Leadership 1945–1982,* Maxwell Air Force Base, Ala.: Air University Press, March 1998, p. 103; Smith, 2013, pp. 66–68.

[43] Futrell, 1989a, p. 553; see, also, the description in Robert Frank Futrell, *Ideas, Concepts, Doctrine: Basic Thinking in the United States Air Force, 1907–1960,* Vol. 2, Maxwell Air Force Base, Ala.: Air University Press, 1989b, p. 713.

[44] Lambeth, 2000, pp. 233–234.

Commanders" and the "Supplement to the Information Policy Letters for Commanders." Beginning in September 1961, the Secretary of the Air Force Office of Information published these letters monthly to provide "concepts, doctrine, facts, references, and suggestions for all Air Force commanders and their staff in meeting their responsibility to advance understanding inside and outside the Air Force."[45] While the letters' content varied widely, they remained a key method to spread ideas for the next several decades.[46]

Occasionally, the Air Force engaged in broader, longer-term planning, perhaps best captured by *Project Forecast*. At the beginning of his tenure, Secretary of the Air Force Eugene Zuckert felt that the Air Force—at that point still dominated by bomber pilots—needed to adapt to the "technological shock" posed by long-range missiles and think through their implications for the service.[47] His method was called *Project Forecast*. Commissioned in 1963 by Zuckert and CSAF General Curtis LeMay and led by the commander of Air Force Systems Command, Gen Bernard Schriever, the project aimed to conduct "a comprehensive study and analysis of the Air Force structure projected into the 1965–1975 time period."[48] Like *Toward New Horizons* of the previous generation, *Project Forecast* looked at a variety of technologies, from materials research to propulsion to electronics, and their implications for everything from continental defense to intelligence gathering to general war.[49] It evaluated not only the technical feasibility of these technologies but also the effect of costs for future Air Force research and development and acquisition efforts.[50] Perhaps one of *Project Forecast*'s most important advantages was that it was relatively free from the strategic bombing lens that dominated Air Force senior leadership's thinking at the time.[51]

Project Forecast shaped the force in both direct and indirect ways. Most directly, *Project Forecast* was about guiding Air Force research and development and procurement efforts for the future. *Project Forecast*, furthermore, also shaped the Air Force more profoundly as an organization. Some *Project Forecast* research team members later authored the August 1964 *Basic Doctrine* and incorporated the former's findings—especially about the need for flexibility, survivability, central direction of command and control, penetration ability, and selective target destruction capability—into the new manual.[52] This *Basic Doctrine* also encouraged the Air

---

[45] Futrell, 1989b, p. 172.

[46] For the use of these letters by various Air Force senior leaders from 1961 through the mid-1980s, see Futrell, 1989b.

[47] Futrell, 1989b, p. 158.

[48] Futrell, 1989b, pp. 158, 228.

[49] Bernard A. Schriever, "Technology and Aerospace Power in the 1970s," *Air University Review*, September–October 1969; Futrell, 1989b, p. 229.

[50] Futrell, 1989b, p. 158.

[51] Worden, 1998, pp. 150–151.

[52] Futrell, 1989b, p. 232.

Force to pursue new technologies—as *Project Forecast* recommended—such as vertical takeoff and landing capabilities. Drawing on *Project Forecast* and lessons learned from the Cuban Missile Crisis, the *Basic Doctrine* redefined victory not only as defeating the enemy but also "the attainment of our specific political objectives" and that "the guiding principle in all crises is to limit the use of force to that compatible with particular conflict issues"—ideas foreign to prevailing bomber culture of the time. Ultimately, in the judgment of historian Robert Futrell, the 1964 *Basic Doctrine* marked a "radical departure from the AFM 1-2 manuals of the 1950s," and this was, in part, the result of *Project Forecast*.[53]

The Air Force also periodically published concept papers on specific strategic issues. For example, in 1962, on the eve of the Vietnam War, the Air Force circulated "The USAF Concept for Limited War."[54] Arguing that wars existed on a spectrum between the Cold War and general wars, with limited war falling somewhere between, it explained the Air Force's role in deterrence and controlling crises. The paper saw raw power as key to controlling these conflicts. In fact, it specifically rejected that limited wars were a distinct entity. It argued, "Since limited war against Communist forces is not a separate entity from general war, our strategy and forces for limited war should not be separated from our overall strategy and force structure."[55] In a sense, the Air Force's strategy for limited wars was a rejection of this category's existence altogether.

In 1965, the Air Force produced "Air Force Doctrine on Air Superiority," another document that thought through the challenges of gaining and maintaining air superiority. In it, the Air Force began to wrestle with some of the Vietnam War's challenges. Specifically, the document recognized that enemy aircraft might be operating from political sanctuaries, decreasing the Air Force's ability to destroy fighters on the ground. As a result, strike aircraft should be capable of dropping external ordnances and transitioning to air-to-air combat quickly when the need arose.[56]

Perhaps the most important intellectual advances, however, happened outside of formal documents altogether, with the work of Col John Boyd. A Korean War fighter pilot and an iconoclast, Boyd believed that Soviet aircraft outmatched American fighters in air-to-air combat. Boyd developed the theory of "energy maneuverability," allowing for comparisons of aircraft maneuverability.[57] He coined the term "OODA [observe, orient, decide, and act] loop" and argued that the key to victory in air combat was getting inside of one's enemy's cycle.[58] According to his *New York Times* obituary, his 1960 study, *Aerial Attack Study*, became the

---

[53] Futrell, 1989b, p. 716.

[54] Futrell, 1989b, p. 56.

[55] Futrell, 1989b, p. 57.

[56] Futrell, 1989b, p. 471.

[57] Robert McG. Thomas, Jr., "Col. John Boyd Is Dead at 70; Advanced Air Combat Tactics," *New York Times*, March 13, 1997; Robert Coram, *Boyd: The Fighter Pilot Who Changed the Art of War*, Boston: Little, Brown and Company, 2002, pp. 327–344; and Frederick W. Kagan, *Finding the Target: The Transformation of the American Military Policy*, New York: Encounter Books, 2006, p. 27.

[58] Thomas, 1997.

"bible of air-to-air combat."[59] On a strategic level, like the earlier airpower advocates, Boyd believed that, if airpower successfully targeted an adversary's center of gravity and cut its lines of communication, airpower could produce strategic victory.[60] Ultimately, Boyd's thinking— according to the *New York Times*—"helped revolutionize American military strategy" and shape a generation of Air Force officers.[61] At the time though, many in the Air Force leadership regarded Boyd as a rebel: a nuisance at best and dangerous at worst.[62]

The Vietnam War and Its Aftermath

Despite Boyd's theories and these early attempts to think through the challenges of the Vietnam War, the conflict proved a scarring experience for the Air Force and for airpower more broadly. Across all four services, some 2,561 aircraft and 3,587 helicopters were lost to enemy fire, and about another 1,200 aircraft and 1,300 helicopters were lost for other reasons.[63] The Air Force alone lost 383 of its 833 F-105s in combat.[64] Kill ratios—the number of hostile-to-friendly aircraft lost—dropped from 8:1 in World War II to between 10:1 and 14:1 during the Korea War to only 2.4:1 in Vietnam.[65] On top of these setbacks, the 1973 Arab-Israeli War showed that the Egyptian army's Soviet-made air-defense systems could neutralize the American-equipped Israeli Air Force's edge in the air.[66] All in all, U.S. command of the air became an increasingly open question.

The Air Force responded to these challenges on multiple fronts. It developed new aircraft, including the F-15 Eagle, F-16 Falcon, A-10 Warthog, EF-111 Raven, and E-3A Sentry.[67] It also trained differently. The Air Force founded the "Aggressor Squadron" at Nellis Air Force Base Nevada in 1972 and later instituted Red Flag exercises in 1975.[68] Attributed to then–Maj Richard "Moody" Suter, who allegedly developed the concept on the back of a cocktail napkin in the Nellis officers' club, Red Flag offered pilots the opportunity to practice "full-scale realistic combat missions" complete with Airborne Warning and Control Systems, downed pilot

---

[59] Thomas, 1997.

[60] Kagan, 2006, p. 111.

[61] Thomas, 1997.

[62] See Coram, 2002. For examples of the Air Force senior leadership's distaste for Boyd, see Coram, 2002, pp. 295, 347–350, 354–355, 369–370.

[63] Kagan, 2006, p. 25; Lambeth, 2000, p. 13.

[64] Lambeth, 2000, p. 13.

[65] Kagan, 2006, p. 25.

[66] Lambeth, 2000, pp. 55–56. For an examination of the effect of the 1973 Arab-Israeli War on American doctrine, see Saul Bronfeld, "Fighting Outnumbered: The Impact of the Yom Kippur War on the U.S. Army," *Journal of Military History*, Vol. 71, No. 2, April 2007.

[67] Kagan, 2006, p. 28.

[68] Kagan, 2006, p. 44–45.

scenarios, and surface-to-air missile sites.[69] Finally, the Air Force also rethought its strategy and role as a service. The September 1971 *Basic Doctrine* included a chapter on special operations and addressed such topics as foreign internal defense, psychological operations, and unconventional warfare. It also was less bullish than previous Air Force documents about the U.S. ability to deter small wars. It warned, "Though it is the keystone of the United States' deterrent posture, strategic sufficiency may not be a credible deterrent against hostile acts by small powers, whether such acts are initiated by those powers alone or while serving as proxies for larger powers."[70]

Later variants of the *Basic Doctrine,* however, proved less introspective. Foreshadowing a later trend, the February 1979 *Basic Doctrine* featured "large type, numerous headlines, catchphrases, line drawings, diagrams, portrait drawings, and numbers of quotations."[71] Indeed, the format was so flashy that "there was an ongoing rumor that the 1979 edition of AFM 1-1 was written to "tell the Air Force Story" rather than as a doctrinal manual to prepare a military force and its commanders for war."[72] Notably, the 1984 variant of the manual dropped the "drawings and flamboyant typography" and reverted back to more-traditional discussions of the principles of wars, the need for air superiority, and the growing importance of space.[73]

The Air Force was only a grudging participant in perhaps the most important strategic concept development of the latter half of the Cold War—AirLand Battle. Learning from the American-equipped Israelis' mishaps fighting the Soviet-equipped Arab armies in the 1973 Arab-Israeli War, the doctrine argued that the army needed to win "the first battle of the next war."[74] Consequently, commanders needed to look beyond the troops immediately to their front and influence the enemy's rear through the coordination of ground and airpower—or AirLand Battle.[75] Despite the fact that the Chiefs of Staff of the Air Force and the Army formally signed onto AirLand Battle in 1983, the Air Force arguably never fully accepted the concept. As Robert Futrell remarks, "The name AirLand Battle implied that there was cooperation and agreement between the Army and the Air Force, but in fact the doctrine was a unilateral development of the Army."[76]

---

[69] Alexander Berger, "Beyond Blue Four: The Past and Future Transformation of Red Flag," *Air and Space Power Journal*, Vol. 19, No. 2, Summer 2005, p. 46; Kagan, 2006, p. 44–45. See, also, Walton S. Moody and Jacob Neufeld, "Modernizing After Vietnam," in Bernard C. Nalty, ed., *Winged Sword, Winged Shield: A History of the United States Air Force 1950–1997*, Vol. II, Washington, D.C.: Air Force History and Museums Program, United States Air Force, 1997, pp. 347–348; Lambeth, 2000, p. 62.

[70] Futrell, 1989b, p. 720.

[71] Futrell, 1989b, p. 735.

[72] Futrell, 1989b, p. 735.

[73] Futrell, 1989b, p. 744.

[74] John L. Romjue, "The Evolution of the AirLand Battle Concept," *Air University Review*, May–June 1984.

[75] Romjue, 1984.

[76] Futrell, 1989b, p. 551.

From the Air Force's standpoint, airpower should achieve a theaterwide effect, not simply be concentrated 30–50 miles in front of the forward line of troops as AirLand Battle seemed to dictate.[77] As airpower scholar and RAND analyst Benjamin Lambeth notes, from the Air Force's standpoint, "the dominance of [AirLand Battle] over the more classic interdiction strategy in air allocation decisions would undermine the ability of the air component commander to mass resources to engage and destroy enemy ground-force concentrations as needed throughout the theater."[78] According to this argument, the Air Force would be able to produce more of an effect if commanders received greater latitude to strike enemy targets wherever they were—not just in front of the Army's ground formations.

Behind the Air Force's reluctance was more than just a debate with the Army over tactics; AirLand Battle struck at the Air Force's very identity as service. At issue was whether the Air Force should primarily support the Army and ground maneuver or whether it should be an independent service capable of producing strategic effect in its own right.[79] For those who believed in a strong independent service, accepting AirLand Battle as a foundational document would be heresy, since it would relegate the Air Force to a subordinate role to the Army and signal "a return to the bad old days of the Army Air Forces."[80]

The Air Force's tepid response to AirLand Battle and uneven relationship with the *Basic Doctrine* marked another trend that was playing out just below the surface: Doctrine was gradually becoming a less important forum for defining the Air Force's role and missions for the future. Doctrine, after all, focused on how the Air Force operates in the present, not how it will need to operate in the future. Instead, defining the Air Force's future increasingly fell to the service's formal long-term strategic planning arm.

In 1977, Secretary of the Air Force John Stetson came into office looking for the Air Force long-range plan.[81] Not finding one, in 1978, Stetson then directed the Air Force to study corporate techniques of long-range planning and whether they could be applied to the service.[82] Led by Brig Gen James P. Albritton, the study looked at a range of examples, including

---

[77] Lambeth, 2000, p. 87.

[78] Lambeth, 2000, p. 89.

[79] Lambeth, 2000, p. 87.

[80] Clark A. Murdock, "Forging the Vision: An Intellectual History of the Post–Cold War Air Force," draft working paper, 2001, p. 4.

[81] Perry McCoy Smith, "Creating a Strategic Vision: The Value of Long-Range Planning," *Air University Review*, September–October 1986.

[82] Jerrod P. Allen, "Institutionalizing Long Range Planning," in Perry M. Smith, Jerrold P. Allen, John H. Stewart II, and F. Douglas Whitehouse, eds., *Creating Strategic Vision: Long-Range Planning for National Security*, Washington, D.C.: National Defense University Press, 1987, p. 31. Some accounts date Stetson's idea for a long-range planning study to 1977; see Smith, 1986; and Perry McCoy Smith, "Long-Range Planning: A National Security Necessity," in Perry M. Smith, Jerrold P. Allen, John H. Stewart II, and F. Douglas Whitehouse, eds., *Creating Strategic Vision: Long-Range Planning for National Security*, Washington D.C.: National Defense University Press, 1987, p. 10.

International Business Machines (IBM), Ford Motor Company, and General Motors Company.[83] While none of these corporations proved a perfect analogy for the Air Force (given its wide set of missions and need to manage many stakeholders, such as Congress and the Executive Branch), the study helped create the Deputy Directorate for Long Range Planning on the Air Staff in 1979.[84] Staffed by about a dozen officers, the directorate was the Air Force's first institutionalized long-range planning arm (as opposed to the ad hoc groups created previously).[85]

The Directorate for Long Range Planning went on to produce a series of documents with varying effect. It began by producing *USAF Global Assessment,* a nearly 200-page document that was "not read cover-to-cover" even by many of the planners themselves but that took each of the issues of interest to the CSAF and the Secretary and tried to look out 15–20 years. The directorate also produced *Planning Guidance Memorandum* and *USAF Planning Guide,* which were less discrete plans and more documents to guide the planning process. Finally, and most importantly, the directorate produced the *USAF Strategy, Force and Capabilities Plan,* which aimed to answer the question of what type of capabilities and structures the Air Force needed to meet national strategic priorities.[86]

Ultimately, the Air Force's decision to enhance its capacity for long-range strategic planning (or at least long-range programmatic planning and resource allocation) proved fortuitous. Starting in the early 1980s, the Air Force also needed to plan how it would spend the extra resources allocated under the Reagan-era defense buildup. To do this, the Air Staff produced *Air Force 2000.* The plan called for investments in three major priorities—stealth, precision, and reliability. With the backing of CSAF Gen Lew Allen and Air Force Secretary Verne Orr, the plan was later socialized with the rest of the Air Force leadership at the Corona conference—the annual gathering of Air Force four-star generals and senior civilian leadership—and also through half-day individual meetings with each of the Air Force four-star generals.[87]

Later, the Air Force released a series of acquisition documents outlining its plans for updating parts of its fleet. It initiated an *Airlift Master Plan* in 1982 (later replaced by the *Integrated Airlift Acquisition Strategy* in 1995) to explain to Congress and the broader policy community how the Air Force intended to transition from the old C-141 to the new C-17 aircraft.[88] The 1984 *Tactical Fighter Roadmap* followed the *Airlift Master Plan* and outlined the

---

[83] Allen, 1987, p. 32.

[84] Allen, 1987, pp. 32–33.

[85] Allen, 1987, p. 33.

[86] Allen, 1987, pp. 34–35.

[87] Interview with a retired Air Force general officer, April 20, 2016.

[88] William T. Y'Blood, "Metamorphosis: The Air Force Approaches the Next Century," in Bernard C. Nalty, ed., *Winged Sword, Winged Shield: A History of the United States Air Force 1950–1997,* Vol. II, Washington, D.C.: Air Force History and Museums Program, 1997, pp. 515–516; see, also, John D. Mayer, Jr. and William P. Myers, *Meeting Future Airlift Requirements: Briefing on Preliminary Analysis of Costs of Alternative Approaches,* Washington, D.C.: Congressional Budget Office, March 1984.

Air Force's fighter needs through 1993, as well as its plans to build to a 40 fighter wing–equivalent structure.[89] The *Bomber Roadmap* came later, in 1992 (later replaced by the 1999 *U.S. Air Force White Paper on Long Range Bombers*),[90] after the Cold War's end prompted the Air Force to refocus the bomber fleet away from the nuclear mission.[91] These documents were part strategy and part public-relations documents, signaling to congressional leaders, industry, and the broader policy audience the direction of the service in the near future. Ultimately, these documents in a practical sense set the parameters for how the Air Force would operate in the future by charting out what capabilities it would buy.

The Air Force also updated older strategic documents. In August 1985, it launched a six-month study—*Project Forecast II*.[92] Designed as a successor to the original 1963 study and conducted by Air Force Systems Command, the study examined the future technological potential for the Air Force to allocate some $2 billion in research and development funding.[93] Ultimately, a 150-person research team evaluated some 1,500 ideas and selected 70 technologies with the most potential—ranging from "super helmets" (which would represent friendly and enemy aircraft, as well as targets, in a cartoon display) and nuclear-powered space "pickup trucks" (to shuttle cargo in and out of space) to, perhaps less futuristic but equally important, advances in composite materials and methods of inserting false data in an adversary's command and control computers.[94]

As with the early periods of its history, some of the most important work on Air Force strategy occurred outside of formal strategy documents, most notably with the writings of Col John Warden. Like Boyd, Warden was a fighter pilot and served in Vietnam as a forward air controller, but he is best known as a strategist. His book *The Air Campaign: Planning for Combat* was published by the National War College in 1988.[95] Like its predecessors, *The Air Campaign* argued that the key to victory in modern war was air superiority.[96] Warden argued,

> Since the German attack on Poland in 1939, no country has won a war in the face
> of enemy air superiority, no major offensive has succeeded against an opponent
> who controlled the air, and no defense has sustained itself against an enemy who

---

[89] Y'Blood, 1997, p. 516; for the congressional reaction, see Ralph Vartabedian, "ATF Funding Faces Cut: Defense Firms Plan to Team for Fighter Job," *Los Angeles Times*, July 2, 1986.

[90] U.S. Air Force, *U.S. Air Force White Paper on Long Range Bombers*, March 1, 1999.

[91] Y'Blood, 1997, p. 517.

[92] Air Force Office of Scientific Research, "A Brief Organizational History," Wright-Patterson Air Force Base website, July 17, 2016.

[93] Peter Grier, "Air Force Peers into Future; Sees 'Smart' Helmets, Radars in Space," *Christian Science Monitor*, April 24, 1986.

[94] Grier, 1986.

[95] John A. Warden III, *The Air Campaign: Planning for Combat*, Washington, D.C.: National Defense University Press, 1988.

[96] Kagan, 2006, p. 113.

had air superiority. Conversely, no state has lost a war while it maintained air superiority, and attainment of air superiority consistently has been a prelude to military victory.[97]

Building on Boyd's theories, Warden also argued that airpower could achieve decisive effect by degrading the adversary's ability to maintain control over its territory and forces.[98]

Warden's theories attracted attention within the Air Force partly for their substance but also because of fortunate timing. For some, Warden became the Air Force's intellectual answer to AirLand Battle, as it was a defense of the service's independence and strategic potential.[99] Gen Michael Dugan—then Deputy Chief of Staff, Plans and Operation on the Air Staff and later CSAF—selected Warden as Deputy Director for Strategy, Doctrine, and Warfighting, a department that contained the Air Force's internal think tank, the Checkmate office.[100] From this perch, Warden helped incorporate his theories into Air Force strategy.[101] More importantly, Warden also served as one of the lead planners of the Gulf War air campaign. As military analyst Fredrick Kagan commented, "Warden had an opportunity offered to not one military theorist in a thousand—he had the chance to put his ideas into almost immediate practice after Saddam Hussein invaded Kuwait on August 2, 1990."[102]

Even after the Gulf War ended, it still was not clear whether Warden was right. For some, the Gulf War validated Warden's theories and "the Gulf War was a harbinger of a 'New Way of War'—what some would even dub 'An American Way of War,'" in which airpower proved decisive.[103] There was, however, another possible reading of the Gulf War. Despite 39 days of bombing, the coalition still needed to launch a ground war to expel Iraqi forces from Kuwait.[104] For Warden personally, Desert Storm proved a mixed experience. He clashed with the commander of Central Command Air Forces, then–Lt Gen Charles A. Horner, and was ultimately sent home from Central Command Air Force headquarters in Riyadh, Saudi Arabia.[105] Still, according to Air Force historian Richard Hallion, Warden's book "assumed the de facto role of doctrinal guide and indeed, air power 'bible,'" overshadowing such official documents as

---

[97] Warden 1988.

[98] Kagan, 2006, p. 141.

[99] Murdock, 2001, p. 4.

[100] Interview with a retired senior Air Force general officer, May 11, 2016.

[101] Faulkenberry, 1996, p. 21.

[102] Kagan, 2006, p. 120.

[103] Murdock, 2001, p. 1.

[104] For an academic discussion of whether airpower was decisive in the Gulf War, see Daryl G. Press, "The Myth of Air Power in the Persian Gulf War and the Future of Warfare," *International Security*, Vol. 26, No. 2, Fall 2001.

[105] For a description of this briefing, see Richard T. Reynolds, *Heart of the Storm: The Genesis of the Air Campaign Against Iraq*, Maxwell Air Force Base, Ala.: Air University Press, January 1995, pp. 120–130.

AFM 1-1 (*Functions and Basic Doctrine of the United States Air Force*), and Warden himself became to the Gulf War what the authors of AWPD 1 were to World War II.[106]

Conclusions from the Period

Ultimately, this brief intellectual history points to a broader conclusion about the Air Force's relationship to strategy, doctrine, and planning documents. Overall, the Air Force has a remarkably rich intellectual history, especially given its comparatively short existence. Beyond a handful of exceptions usually focused on projecting the future of technology, such as *Toward New Horizons* and *Project Forecast*, the most influential pieces were often the work of individuals—from Mitchell and LeMay to Boyd and Warden—and not the work of a deliberate, bureaucratic planning process. In many cases, it took a forceful civilian leader to push the Air Force to embrace long-range planning, as with Zuckert in the case of *Project Forecast* or Stetson with the creation of the *Long-Range Planning Directorate*. Even the many versions of the *Basic Doctrine* seem largely to reflect—rather than drive—strategic thinking at the time.

Although it may not have been particularly revolutionary, Air Force strategic planning still performed three important functions during this period. Some documents—such as *Air Force 2000,* the "Tactical Fighter Roadmap," and the "Airlift Master Plan"—helped guide the service's resource allocation. This was no small task. In fact, some of the influential documents—*Toward New Horizons* and *Project Forecast*—were primarily scientific reviews seeking to answer the questions about what technology would shape the future of airpower in the years to come. Other documents—such as *Initial Postwar Air Force*—helped define how the then–Army Air Force should be structured. Perhaps most importantly, these documents slowly but surely helped carve out a bureaucratic role for the Air Force as a separate but coequal branch of service. In this sense, all the doctrinal documents, be it FM 100-20 or the later iterations of *Basic Doctrine*, played a crucial if understated role by etching into a semipermanent document the Air Force's role and mission. This idea—of using strategy to define the service's identity—would later become increasingly important as the Air Force entered the post–Cold War period.

---

[106] Hallion, 1992, p. 118.

4. Air Force Strategy from 1990 to the Present

In 1990, the U.S. military faced a strategic crossroads. The Berlin War had fallen, the Soviet Union was collapsing, and the Cold War was ending. As a result, the guiding strategic imperative—how to defeat a Soviet invasion—was rapidly becoming irrelevant, but it was not clear what was to come next. Without a clearly defined, credible threat on the horizon, the military faced the prospect of massive budget cuts, as politicians wanted to reap a "peace dividend" and redirect resources to domestic spending. The services needed to define their role in the post–Cold War age, and they needed to do so quickly. What that argument would be for the Air Force in particular, however, was not immediately clear. The service's leadership was divided between those who saw the Air Force's primary role as providing tactical air support to the Army and those who saw airpower as a tool to win wars in its own right.[1] For many airmen, the Air Force seemed to be a service that had lost its way.[2]

An internal Air Force analysis, written by then–Lt Col Michael Hayden for then-CSAF Gen Larry Welch and circulated in fall 1989, argued that, as "an institution, we have unwittingly crippled our capacity to deal with the realities of the late 20th century even though these realities in any objective sense should be less threatening to the Air Force than to any other service."[3] The paper cited senior Air Force leaders who argued that the service focused on systems rather missions.[4] Moreover, the paper posited that, despite this equipment focus, the Air Force resisted technological change. It noted that, after a joint task force recommended more unmanned systems, "[t]he Air Staff 'circled the wagons' around the inviolable role of the manned penetrator and the task force's recommendations were diluted."[5]

Above all, the paper argued that the Air Force lost its identity. In a backhanded swipe at the of AirLand Battle advocates, the paper suggested that the Air Force delegated its identity to others: "When the commander of TAC declares his forces are there *to support the Army in achieving its battlefield objectives*, the Air Force (rightly or wrongly) abdicates the definition

---

[1] In 1988, Gen John "Mike" Loh, then the commander of Tactical Air Command (TAC), said, "Tactical aviators have two primary jobs—to provide air defense for the North American continent and support the Army in achieving its battlefield objectives." To service parochialists, this statement seemed to relegate the Air Force to subordinate status." (Murdock, 2001, p. 4)

[2] Perhaps another example of this overall dissatisfaction with the state of the service was an Air Force "brown paper" circulated around the service in 1991. Widely distributed within the service and eventually leaked to the press, the anonymously authored paper mocked the Air Force fighter pilot–dominated culture. Embedded within the paper was a serious critique of Air Force culture—which faced a growing divide between the fighter pilot wing and the rest of the service (Smith, 2013, pp. 108–109).

[3] "A View of the Air Force Today," brown paper, Fall 1989, p. 3.

[4] "A View of the Air Force Today," 1989, p. 6.

[5] "A View of the Air Force Today," 1989, p. 14.

about much of what it is about to the Army."[6] The paper also noted that "there is no contemporary Air Force statement comparable to the integrating vision of the Maritime Strategy or AirLand battle."[7] Ultimately, the paper concluded the following:

> Carl Builder of RAND was one of the most alarmist people we talked to, declaring he believed "100% that the Air Force as an institution had lost a sense of identity." Conversely, he was also one of the most optimistic. Of the three Services, he said, the Air Force was the most capable of appreciating the problem and acting upon it. . . . We share both Builder's optimism and his strong sense of urgency.[8]

Over the next 25 years, strategic documents attempted to answer the paper's challenge and give the Air Force its missing sense of identity.[9] Along the way, they accomplished several other critical objectives as well: justifying and allocating the Air Force's budget; shaping and structuring the force; and, perhaps more importantly, encouraging a dialogue about the future of the service.

Global Reach—Global Power and Blueprints for the Objective Air Force (1990)

The first of the major Air Force strategic documents of the post–Cold War period was also, perhaps, the most controversial and influential. In June 1990, Secretary of the Air Force Donald Rice unveiled the white paper, *The Air Force and the U.S. National Security: Global Reach—Global Power*.[10] A trained engineer and economist, and the former president and chief executive officer of the RAND Corporation, Rice brought an academic flavor to his time as Secretary, along with a deep knowledge of Air Force institutional issues.[11] When the academic journal *International Security* published a critique of the new B-2 bomber, Rice penned a 28-page

---

[6] "A View of the Air Force Today," 1989, p. 10 (emphasis in the original).

[7] "A View of the Air Force Today," 1989, p. 7.

[8] "A View of the Air Force Today," 1989, p. 28.

[9] More recently, Paula Thornhill argues that the Air Force has had not one but five different cultural narratives over its history and has struggled to find a single unifying narrative. See Paula G. Thornhill, *"Over Not Through": The Search for a Strong, Unified Culture for America's Airmen*, Santa Monica, Calif.: RAND Corporation, OP-386-AF, 2012.

[10] Glen W. Moorhead III, *Global Reach—Global Power and the USAF Tactical Air Forces*, Carlisle Barracks, Pa.: U.S. Army War College, April 15, 1991, p. 2.

[11] One retired general officer remarked, because of Rice's time overseeing RAND and Project AIR FORCE, "Rice knew more about Air Force than three and four stars because he studied it from macro level rather than stovepipe perspective. He is by nature analytic, thinking about the future" (interview with a retired senior Air Force general officer, May 11, 2016).

journal article in response.[12] Perhaps unsurprisingly then, Rice later wrote his *Global Reach—Global Power* white paper to help guide the Air Force through a period of strategic uncertainty.

Rice's white paper served multiple goals. On a basic level, it attempted to confront the real concerns posed by the end of the Reagan build up and start of the post–Cold War drawn down.[13] As the United States attempted to reap a "peace dividend," Air Force funding declined by 34 percent, active duty personnel contracted by 27 percent, and base installations were cut by 24 percent over a ten-year period from 1986 to 1995.[14] Gen Merrill McPeak—who became CSAF right after his predecessor, Gen Michael J. Dugan, was fired for talking too openly about what airpower could do in the Gulf War and shortly after *Global Reach—Global Power*'s release—downplayed these budget influences on strategy.[15] He noted, "We would want to pursue these initiatives even if there were no budget pressure to do so," but undeniably, these issues still lurked in the background.[16] Even McPeak acknowledged that *Global Reach—Global Power* provided "the framework for corporate strategic planning. It guides us in resource allocation, providing the conceptual foundation on which we build programs that produce the Air Force of tomorrow."[17]

Global Reach—Global Power went beyond budgets, however: It attempted to define Air Force identity. In a June 1992 speech, McPeak recounted,

> At one level, *Global Reach—Global Power* is a statement of first principles. It asserts that we are an air- and space-faring nation and describes how this fact is central to achieving our national objectives. But it is also more than this. *Global Reach—Global Power* describes how airpower contributes to national security, highlighting the attributes—speed, range, flexibility, precision, lethality—that, in combination, set us apart from other purveyors of military force.[18]

Global Reach—Global Power captured the Air Force's uniqueness among the services. "Air, naval and land forces are fundamentally and necessarily different," McPeak argued. "For them, air operations are seen as an extension of surface activity, needed to make possible safer, more

---

[12] See Michael E. Brown, "The U.S. Manned Bomber and Strategic Deterrence in the 1990s," *International Security*, Vol. 14, No. 2, Fall 1989; and Donald B. Rice, "The Manned Bomber and Strategic Deterrence: The U.S. Air Force Perspective," *International Security*, Vol. 15, No. 1, Summer 1990b.

[13] One of the authors, then-Col David Deptula, argued that one of the document's main intended audiences was the Defense Planning Resource Board for precisely this reason (Murdock, 2001, p. 3).

[14] Michael Barzelay and Colin Campbell, *Preparing for the Future: Strategic Planning in the U.S. Air Force*, Washington, D.C.: Brooking Institution Press, July 31, 2003, p. 37.

[15] John M. Broder, "Air Force Chief Fired by Cheney," *Los Angeles Times*, September 18, 1990.

[16] Rebecca Grant, "End of the Cold War Air Force," *Air Force Magazine*, July 2012, p. 42. Importantly, media accounts at the time argued that *Global Reach—Global Power* provided the basis for the defense reductions. See Patrick E. Tyler, "Military Chiefs Detail Plans to Cut Troops, Weapons," *Washington Post*, May 12, 1990, p. A1.

[17] Speech at Airpower Dining-In at Maxwell Air Force Base, Alabama, June 19, 1992, in Merrill A. McPeak, *Selected Works of Merrill A. McPeak: 1990–1994*, Maxwell Air Force Base, Ala.: Air University Press, August 1995, p. 154

[18] Speech at Airpower Dining-In, Maxwell Air Force Base, Alabama, June 19, 1992, in McPeak, 1995, p. 154.

effective maneuvers on land or at sea. We, on the other hand, seek to control and exploit air and space—not to facilitate operations somewhere else but to achieve national objectives in and through this dimension."[19] Drafted by staff officers who were intellectual disciples of Warden, *Global Reach—Global Power* pushed back against AirLand Battle and the notion that the Air Force would play a supporting role to the Army. Instead, the white paper argued that airpower could be an end unto itself.[20] As one Air Force senior leader recounted, "the Air Force had a heart, but [with *Global Reach—Global Power*] I wanted to articulate its soul."[21]

As a document, *Global Reach—Global Power* was intentionally short (at just 15 pages, with a two-paragraph introduction), no photographs, and only a handful of diagrams.[22] In contrast to later documents that tended to be cosigned by the Secretary and the CSAF, *Global Reach—Global Power* only bears Rice's signature, not the then-CSAF Gen Larry Welch's, although Welch saw the document before its publication.[23] Its message was similarly simple: The paper stressed the Air Force's role in power projection both in terms of striking long distances and in rapid airlift and refueling capabilities.[24] With the Cold War's end and overseas base closures on the horizon, *Global Reach—Global Power* argued that "rapid power projection from the continental United States [CONUS] would be tomorrow's *soup de jour*—and the Air Force was already there."[25]

Global Reach—Global Power reverberated throughout the force. Then–Air Force Maj and later Maj Gen Barbara Faulkenberry recounts, "The concept of 'Global Reach—Global Power' certainly took the Air Force by storm. Soon it could be seen on hangars, placards, and in publications. There were even plans to produce a bumper sticker with the phrase."[26] There are several reasons for *Global Reach—Global Power*'s popularity. As already mentioned, it came when the United States was at a strategic crossroads with the end of Cold War, and the white paper provided direction. *Global Reach—Global Power* also provided a retort to the Air Force's seeming loss of bureaucratic ground to the Army in AirLand Battle. Finally, *Global Reach—*

---

[19] Speech at Airpower Dining-In at Maxwell Air Force Base, Alabama, June 19, 1992, in McPeak, 1995, p. 158. Importantly, some media accounts argue that this distinction was also directly tied to protecting Air Force budget interests. For example, the *Washington Post*'s Patrick Tyler argued, "The title [of *Global Reach—Global Power*] reflects the competitive assertion that Air Force, not the Navy, should assume a greater share of the 'power projection' mission in the future." Similarly, Don Oberdorfer, also of the *Washington Post*, argued that *Global Reach—Global Power* was the Air Force's attempt to respond to the Army's claim to the mantle of being the nation's power projection force (Don Oberdorfer, "Strategy for Solo Superpower: Pentagon Looks to 'Regional Contingencies,'" *Washington Post*, May 19, 1991, p. A1).

[20] Murdock, 2001, pp. 4, 5.

[21] Interview with a former senior Air Force civilian leader, September 16, 2016.

[22] Rice, 1990a; and interview with a retired senior Air Force general officer, May 11, 2016.

[23] Interview with a retired senior Air Force general officer, May 11, 2016.

[24] Rice, 1990a, pp. 8, 11.

[25] Murdock, 2001, p. 6.

[26] Faulkenberry, 1996, pp. 17–18.

Global Power was novel: It was the first vision statement of its kind.[27] A former senior Air Force general officer recounts how at last *Global Reach—Global Power* provided something the Air Force "could stand for," a document to unite the services' different tribes under a single banner.[28] Whatever the true reason, if readership is one of the first measures of effectiveness, *Global Reach—Global Power* passes with flying colors, as it certainly gained the Air Force's attention.

Global Reach—Global Power's fame was also aided by a chance turn of events. In August 1990, just months after the paper's release, Iraq invaded Kuwait, and the defense establishment turned its attention to more-concrete tasks, namely planning for Operations Desert Shield and Desert Storm.[29] According to Air Force strategist Clark Murdock, "Rarely has a vision document been so rapidly reinforced by events, but as the evolving intellectual debate within the Air Force would demonstrate, it was the punchy bumper sticker—'Global Reach—Global Power'—that has stuck [and] not the actual content of the vision."[30] Desert Storm, after all, featured some 1,624 B-52 sorties over Iraq—flow by aircraft from bases in Louisiana, Great Britain, Spain, and Diego Garcia atoll and throughout the Middle East.[31]

Despite its seeming validation during the Gulf War, *Global Reach—Global Power* still proved controversial. First, some faulted the process by which it was developed. While the document was reviewed by the CSAF and his staff, Michael Barzelay and Colin Campbell argue that the plan was primarily the outgrowth of Rice's thinking but lacked buy-in from the Air Force overall.[32] Others criticize *Global Reach—Global Power*'s execution. Faulkenberry noted, "Though studies attempted to quantify the Air Force's physical ability to provide its promised global power and reach, no attempt was made to see what effect the vision statement had on the force internally or if the message was perceived as intended."[33] Still others criticized *Global Reach—Global Power*'s content. Some Air Force officers dismissed it as "advertising, a coffee

---

[27] Murdock, 2001, p. 4.

[28] Interview with a retired senior Air Force general officer, September 1, 2016.

[29] Barzley and Campbell, 2003, p. 28.

[30] Murdock, 2001, p .7.

[31] Hallion, 1992, pp. 163, 218.

[32] Barzelay and Campbell, 2003, p. 43; and interview with a former senior Air Force civilian leader, September 16, 2016.

[33] Faulkenberry, 1996, p. 18. For example, the Air Force Center for Studies and Analyses publishes a paper on how *Global Reach—Global Power* should influence Secretary of Defense Dick Cheney's *Major Aircraft Review* (including the C-17, B-2, advanced attack aircraft, and advanced tactical fighter) and ongoing congressional budget fights. See Gregory S. Parnell, Richard L. Eilers, Philip A. Richard, Steve P. Doucet, John A. Rolando, Larry D. Autry, Gregg M. Burgess, Patricia M. Fornes, Patrick J. Thomas, and John L. Burkhart, *Methodology for Analyzing Global Reach—Global Power*, white paper, Washington, D.C.: Air Force Center for Studies and Analyses, the Pentagon, October 11, 1990, p. 2.

table document," while others accused it of marginalizing space, information, and nonlethal operations.[34]

Perhaps the more cutting critique of *Global Reach—Global Power* was that it did not present a practical plan. For example, RAND political scientist Alan Vick argues, "This USAF document [*Global Reach—Global Power*] read more like the White House National Security Strategy or Joint Chiefs of Staff National Military Strategy than a service document, describing and illustrating how the USAF had and would contribute to achieving diverse U.S. national security objectives."[35] While the paper provided a vision for a "garrison force with extensive overseas basing rights to a smaller CONUS-based 'expeditionary force,'" it provided few specifics.[36]

The most damning critique of all, however, was that neither airpower's successes during the Gulf War nor *Global Reach—Global Power* spared the Air Force from the budget battles that followed. Immediately after Desert Storm, the George H. W. Bush administration called for a 25-percent reduction across all the services as part of a post–Cold War draw down.[37] The other side of the aisle was similarly intent on cutting the Air Force. In July 1992, Chairman of the Senate Armed Services Committee Sam Nunn said on the Senate floor, "we're the only military in the world with four air forces . . . [and] this redundancy and duplication is costing us billions every year."[38] Then–Arkansas Governor Bill Clinton endorsed Nunn's comment and pledged that, as President, he would "reduce redundancies, save billions of dollars and get better teamwork."[39]

Ironically, thanks to these budget shortfalls, some accuse the Air Force of cutting some the very systems that provided "global reach" and "global power." For example, defense analyst Gene Myers labeled Rice's paper as "a stillborn doctrine" because of the gap between the strategy's proposed means and available resources.[40] He notes that, despite Rice and McPeak preaching "global reach" in theory, in practice, the Air Force cut long-range bombers (particularly the B-1 and B-2 fleets), leaving it with F-15s, F-16s, and F-117s, all of which

---

[34] Faulkenberry, 1996, p. 26. Similarly, then–Lt Col Phillip Meilinger argues that the Air Force strategy more broadly has been unable to envision the new world order: "Unfortunately, it is ill-prepared to move into the new world; in fact, the Air Force was becoming increasingly unable to deal with the old world. Since the end of the Vietnam war, our service has been uncertain of its overall purpose and unsure of the fundamental principles underlying air power" (Meilinger, 1992).

[35] Alan Vick, *Proclaiming Airpower: Air Force Narratives and American Public Opinion from 1917 to 2014*, Santa Monica, Calif.: RAND Corporation, RR-1044-AF, 2015, pp. 70–71.

[36] Moorhead, 1991, p. 15; see, also, Barzelay and Campbell, 2003, p. 51.

[37] Murdock, 2001, p. 8.

[38] Thomas P. Ehrhard, *An Air Force Strategy for the Long Haul*, Washington, D.C.: Center for Strategic and Budgetary Assessments, 2009, p. 2.

[39] Michael R. Gordon, "Report by Powell Challenges Calls to Revise Military," *New York Times*, December 31, 1992.

[40] Gene Myers, "Global Reach—Global Power: A Stillborn Doctrine," *Defense Analysis*, Vol. 8, No. 3, 1992, p. 319.

require "runways within 500–600 miles of their targets to be really effective."[41] (By contrast, the Air Force leadership at the time countered that they preserved much of these capabilities, proven by the fact that the B-2 fleets flown from Missouri equipped with the newly developed Joint Direct Attack Munitions, would strike some of initial blows during the 1999 Kosovo Air Campaign).[42]

Another, more concrete document was needed to help make *Global Reach—Global Power* practical and to guide the service through the postwar period of budget austerity. McPeak believed in *Global Reach—Global Power*'s message about range and precision, but he felt the Air Force needed a more definitive set of long-range plans. As a result, he began work on *Blueprints for the Objective Air Force* with the service.[43] In McPeak's words, "This very important work describes where we are headed (and, maybe more important, where we are not headed) with our organizational structure. It 'creates facts' and therefore helps us believe that the problem is boundable, manageable."[44] The document outlined his vision for the structure of the Air Force but also practical considerations about where to station units and which units to keep and which to disband.

Processwise, however, *Blueprints for the Objective Air Force* was very similar to *Global Reach—Global Power*. McPeak believed that he—not the Air Staff—was primarily responsible for long-range planning and that he should be the main driving force behind it. [45] For better or worse, it was less a consensus document of common wisdom and more the CSAF's vision for where the service should head in the future. If *Global Reach—Global Power* was Rice's document, *Blueprints* was McPeak's.

McPeak and Rice soon implemented widespread reforms. Inside headquarters, the Air Staff was reorganized to better align with *Global Reach—Global Power*'s vision, but larger moves were in store for the rest of the service.[46] Military Airlift Command became Air Mobility Command. TAC folded into the newly formed Air Combat Command. Strategic Air Command was abolished and divided its assets into Air Mobility Command and the newly formed Air Combat Command, while a new joint "U.S. Strategic Command," a new functional combatant command, assumed the nuclear mission.[47] Air Systems Command and Air Logistics Command

---

[41] Myers, 1992, p. 320.

[42] Interview with a former Air Force senior leader, September 16, 2016.

[43] Interview with a retired senior Air Force general officer, April 14, 2016.

[44] McPeak, 1995, p. xxiii.

[45] Interview with a retired senior Air Force general officer, April 14, 2016.

[46] Interview with a retired senior Air Force general officer, May 11, 2016.

[47] Some analysts argue that the abolishment of Strategic Air Command caused the Air Force to lose focus on the nuclear mission and, particularly, on the Intercontinental Ballistic Missile force. Indeed, the Intercontinental Ballistic Missile force would decades later be plagued with a series of scandals, including cheating on tests and drug use, eventually pushing the Air Force to create a new Global Strike Command in 2009. See Adam Lowther, "A Year Later: Responding to Problems in the ICBM Force," *Bulletin of the Atomic Scientists*, February 12, 2015.

folded into Air Force Material Command.[48] Additionally, smaller commands—including Air Force Communications Command, Air University, Alaskan Air Command, and Air Force Intelligence Command—were reorganized and lost their major command status.[49] Rice and McPeak also eliminated general officer billets on staff and put brigadier generals in command of 65 of the 115 air wings.[50] The reforms reflected the Goldwater-Nichols Act vision of commands working directly for the Combatant Commanders as part of the Joint Force, and much of the acquisition authority was centralized under DoD.[51] The reforms, however, also left the Air Force with a flatter structure and its projection capability under a small number of major commands, thus better enabling the Air Force to fulfill its goal of having global reach and global power.[52]

Rice eventually returned to strategy toward the end of his tenure as Secretary of the Air Force and published an updated *Global Reach—Global Power: The Evolving Air Force Contribution to National Security* in December 1992.[53] This version was less about breaking new ground and more about "taking stock about what we had learned and reasserting the basics."[54] As Faulkenberry recounts,

> Less attention seems to have been expended on disseminating the message, probably due to the "update" sense of the document. Public Affairs provided copies to politicians, the media and key defense corporations and civil leaders. Again, no attempt was made to measure the effectiveness of the message. Secretary Rice stepped down in January 1993 and attention turned to a new secretary and other issues.[55]

Despite the lack of fanfare for the updated message, there is no denying that Rice and McPeak reshaped the Air Force dramatically during their tenures. Indeed, many of their reforms still shape the Air Force today. Much of this was because of the unique set of historical

---

[48] Grant, 2012, pp. 40–41.

[49] Grant, 2012, p. 44.

[50] Grant, 2012, p. 43. The move had major second-order effects. Some support roles—such as intelligence—were left with only a handful of general officer billets and understrength at the senior levels, compared with the Air Force's sister services (interview with a retired senior Air Force general officer, May 11, 2016).

[51] According to McPeak, the logic of the reorganization was twofold. First, it centralized most of the Air Force's combat capabilities under Air Combat Command. Second, on the support side, the reorganization also partially responded to the Goldwater-Nichols Act of 1986, which stripped much of the acquisition authority from the services. See Grant, 2012, pp. 42, 44; also Hallion, 1992, p. 259.

[52] See Harry Levins, "Flying High . . . 'Big Bomb' Takes a Back Seat in the New Air Force," *St. Louis Post-Dispatch*, September 22, 1991, p. 1C; Hallion, 1992, p. 265.

[53] Air Force Association, *Global Reach—Global Power: The Evolving Air Force Contribution to National Security*, Arlington, Va., December 1992.

[54] Interview with a former Air Force senior leader, September 16, 2016.

[55] Faulkenberry, 1996, p. 20. Another retired senior Air Force general officer agreed: "I don't think it accomplished a whole lot. It was the next regime wanting to update and incorporate Desert Storm lessons" (interview with a retired senior Air Force general officer, May 12, 2016).

circumstances stemming from the end of the Cold War and the beginning of the unipolar age.[56] And yet, parts of these changes are at least summed up in *Global Reach—Global Power*.

Global Presence (1995)

After Rice left as Secretary of the Air Force, the onus for Air Force strategy informally passed from the Secretary to the CSAF.[57] In August 1994, the Air Force began work on another strategy, *Global Presence*.[58] McPeak's successor, Gen Ronald R. Fogleman, and the new Air Force Secretary Sheila Widnall completed the strategy. Unlike the *Blueprints for the Objective Force*, *Global Presence* did not reorganize the Air Force nor did it attract the same media attention. Indeed, Maj Gen Robert Linhard, then the director of Air Force planning, told journalists that *Global Presence* "doesn't point toward any big changes in the service's mix of aircraft or its spending patterns."[59] Rather, *Global Presence* had a narrower purpose, namely to rethink the role of the Air Force now that the post–Cold War period heralded a return to more of a garrison posture and to stake out the Air Force's role in American military engagement abroad.[60] Specifically, it attempted to convince policymakers that the Air Force was a cheaper but equally productive alternative to sending an aircraft carrier overseas to show the flag.[61] Indeed, Fogleman even "recolored from 'blue,' highlighting the role the Air Force plays in the nationally directed presence mission, to 'purple,' emphasizing the role of airpower in a 'common core mission.'"[62]

Intentional or not, *Global Presence* succeeded in rankling the Navy and the Marine Corps, which saw it as a threat to their traditional roles.[63] In 1992, the Navy had released its own strategy, *Forward . . . From the Sea*. It argued, "The Cold War may be over, but the need for American leadership and commensurate military capability endures. Many of our most vital

---

[56] Indeed, the Air Force's internal look occurred within the context of a wider push to reevaluate the size of the U.S military and posture post–Cold War, beginning with DoD's *Bottom Up Review* published in 1993. See Les Aspin, *Report of the Bottom-Up Review*, Washington, D.C.: U.S. Department of Defense, October 1993.

[57] Murdock, 2001, p. 9. The shift in the onus for strategic planning from the service secretary to CSAF was partly because of personality. As already mentioned, Rice was in some ways uniquely suited for the task given his background in Air Force strategy from his days at RAND. There were also institutional reasons. After Rice left, McPeak took a "never again" approach to letting the Secretary dictate the Air Force vision and shifted some of the Secretary's planning staff back under the CSAF (interview with a retired senior Air Force general officer, May 11, 2016).

[58] Faulkenberry, 1996, p. 24. See, also, Sheila E. Widnall and Ronald R. Fogleman, *Global Presence*, Washington, D.C.: National Defense University, Institute for National Strategic Studies, Fort Lesley J. McNair, 1995.

[59] Thomas E. Ricks, "Air Force Says It Can Offer 'Presence' in Peacetime at Lower Cost than Navy," *Wall Street Journal*, February 27, 1995.

[60] Faulkenberry, 1996, p. 25; and interview with a former Air Force general officer, June 27, 2016.

[61] Ricks, 1995.

[62] Faulkenberry, 1996, p. 24.

[63] Y'Blood, 1997, p. 515.

interests remain overseas where the Navy and the Marine Corps are prepared for new challenges—*forward* deployed, **ready** for combat, and **engaged** to preserve the peace."[64] *Global Presence* seemed to argue that the Air Force could perform the Navy and Marine Corps' forward engagement function, both by flying aircraft in and out when needed and through "virtual means," such as with space and information assets.[65] Then–Chief of Naval Operations ADM Jeremy Boorda told reporters that he was blindsided by the paper: "I didn't know they [the Air Force] were doing this." He dismissed the idea that Air Force aircraft could substitute for carrier strike groups, saying "we're never going to have a 'virtual Navy.'"[66]

In fairness, the reaction to *Global Presence* must be viewed in context. In 1993, Congress mandated a national review of the services' roles in the post–Cold War period. With service budgets at stake, the "Commission on Roles and Missions of the Armed Forces" proved a politically charged affair.[67] The Air Force presentation—spearheaded by then–recently retired McPeak—unabashedly pushed for a larger role for the Air Force in airlift, space, deep strike, and other domains, a move that was interpreted by the other services as "all but a declaration of interservice war."[68] In fact, the Army's point person on the Commission, LTG Jay Garner, even summed up the Air Force's position as "Air Force *uber alles*."[69] In this atmosphere, such documents as *Global Presence* struck an already-raw nerve.

Still, *Global Presence* accomplished its admittedly narrow task. Faulkenberry argues that *Global Presence* was a "successful white paper," since the Commission on Roles and Missions of the Armed Forces' *Directions on Defense* June 1995 argued that DoD should "experiment with new approaches for achieving overseas presence objectives."[70] It is impossible to say whether the commission would have reached this recommendation simply with McPeak's forceful, if impolitic, advocacy without *Global Presence*, but the commission's recommendation was a bureaucratic victory for the Air Force, albeit a politically costly one. As Murdock notes, Fogleman, who came into office wanting to set a less confrontational tone than McPeak, "must have been chagrined by the Navy's reaction to 'Global Presence.'"[71]

Global Presence's bureaucratic victory teaches a broader point: In general, service strategies prove effective if they are nested inside the broader DoD perspective and national security environment at the time. *Global Presence* came out at a time when DoD looked to increase its

---

[64] U.S. Department of the Navy, *Forward . . . From the Sea*, Washington, D.C., 1992 (emphasis in original).

[65] Murdock, 2001, p. 10.

[66] Ricks, 1995.

[67] Lambeth, 2000, p. 275.

[68] Lambeth, 2000, p. 278.

[69] Lambeth, 2000, p. 278.

[70] Faulkenberry, 1996, p. 25. U.S. Department of Defense, "A Commission on Roles and Missions," June 1995, pp. 2–21.

[71] Murdock, 2001, p. 11.

worldwide military engagement, but without the implicit price tag. *Global Presence* gave DoD and Congress (albeit indirectly through the Roles and Missions Commission) such an alternative.

Global Engagement (1996)

Fogleman and Widnall's next document, *Global Engagement: A Vision for the 21st-Century Air Force*, served multiple purposes. According to its stated purpose, *Global Engagement* aimed to "forge a new vision that will guide [the Air Force] into the 21st Century."[72] Politically, Widnall and Fogleman worried that Congress might strip the Air Force of its space mission and form a separate service unless "it geared up culturally and programmatically for greater emphasis on space."[73] It also was a response to the fear that the Air Force was being excluded from interservice dialogues.[74] Others claim that *Global Engagement* came from Fogleman's inherent belief in the value of long-term strategic planning and his desire to leave his mark on the Air Force.[75] Whatever the true reason for its creation, *Global Engagement* is commonly cited as the benchmark for Air Force strategic documents in the post–Cold War period.

Fogleman believed that "before you can get your senior leadership to sell anything, they've got to believe it," and he developed a process to gain their buy-in.[76] Particularly after the Goldwater-Nichols reforms, which stripped the service chiefs of some of their institutional power, Fogleman needed support from his fellow senior general officers. He appointed a lieutenant general as director of the Long-Range Planning Board of Directors to underscore the effort's importance. Fogleman then insisted that that the deputy commanders of all the major component commands—rather than lower-ranking staff officers—attend the planning sessions. Fogleman then extended the Corona conference from three to five days in October 1996. At the conference, the Long-Range Planning Board presented some 16 briefing papers for the senior leadership's approval, thereby securing buy-in for the concepts embedded within *Global Engagement* across the service.[77] Drawing on lessons from the conference, the Air Force published *Global Engagement* in 1996, signed by Fogleman and Widnall.

Global Engagement made three principal claims. First, it stated that, "[i]n the twenty-first century, it will be possible to find, fix or track and target anything that moves on the surface of the earth. This emerging reality will change the conduct of warfare and the role of air and space

---

[72] Ronald R. Fogleman and Sheila E. Widnall, *Global Engagement: A Vision for the 21st-Century Air Force*, 1996.

[73] Campbell, 2002, p. 438; Barzelay and Campbell, 2003, p. 1; and interview with a senior Air Force leader, May 5, 2016.

[74] Barzelay and Campbell, 2003, p. 35.

[75] Campbell, 2002, p. 425; and interview with a former Air Force general officer, June 27, 2016.

[76] Barzelay and Campbell, 2003, p. 1.

[77] Barzelay and Campbell, 2003, pp. 44, 46, 55.

power."[78] With this statement, *Global Engagement* asserted that airpower's primary role was no longer supporting ground forces, but a tool to win wars in its own right.[79] The second claim redefined the relationship between airpower and space-based assets. As *Global Engagement* proclaims, "We are now transitioning from an *air and space* force on an evolutionary path to a *space and air* force."[80] Third, and perhaps most importantly, *Global Engagement* tried to define Air Force culture. The document made the Air Force Academy's core values—integrity first, service before self, and excellence in all we do—core Air Force values.[81] *Global Engagement* also tried to define the six Air Force core competencies—rapid global mobility, precision engagement, global attack, air and space superiority, information superiority, and agile combat support.[82]

At the end of the day, *Global Engagement* proved mostly successful. On the technological level, Fogleman and *Global Engagement*, arguably, successfully spurred the Air Force to more fully embrace unmanned aerial vehicles (UAVs).[83] Similarly, *Global Engagement*'s statement about being able to "find, fix or track and target anything" would be a harbinger of the kill chain that would define the service's approach to operation.

Perhaps more important, however, were *Global Engagement*'s strides in defining a coherent, unified Air Force culture. The Air Force core competencies and its core values outlined in *Global Engagement* remain largely the same today.[84] The values and competencies provided a first step in uniting the Air Force's different tribes and giving the Air Force a coherent identity.

Global Engagement also blunted some of the calls from external audiences to create a separate space force, albeit at a cost. Peter Hays and Karl Mueller suggest that the document "raised more issues than it resolved," arguing that "[m]any saw it as a divisive vision because it clearly seemed to promote space separatism without providing much guidance concerning critical issues such as the rationale or timing for the Air Force's evolution to a space and air force."[85] Similarly, James Smith, a retired Air Force officer turned Air Force Academy faculty, argued that the concept "fractured" the service and said, "Air Force officers are, overall and

---

[78] Kagan, 2006, p. 230.

[79] Barzelay and Campbell, 2003, p. 35. For a description of the lingering doubts by some in the Air Force about the ability of airpower to win wars even after the Gulf War, see Meilinger, 1992.

[80] Fogleman and Widnall, 1996 (emphasis in the original).

[81] Interview with an Air Force senior leader, May 5, 2016.

[82] Fogleman and Widnall, 1996.

[83] Fogleman and Widnall, 1996; Thomas P. Ehrhard, *Air Force UAVs: The Secret History*, Arlington, Va.: The Mitchell Institute, 2010, pp. 47–57.

[84] Murdock, 2001, p. 17; and U.S. Air Force, *Air Force Future Operating Concept: A View of the Air Force in 2035*, Washington, D.C., September 2015, p. 12.

[85] Hays and Mueller, 2001, p. 37.

particularly within the rated community, not yet ready to make that transition."[86] In his study of the Air Force's relationship to space, airpower analyst Benjamin Lambeth argued that, despite *Global Engagement's* statements about becoming a "space and air force,"

> both friends and critics nonetheless expressed concern over the extent to which that service's leaders were genuinely committed to moving the Air Force into space and, indeed, whether the Air Force was even the appropriate service to inherit the mantle of military space exploitation to begin with.[87]

Ultimately, he concluded,

> although one can readily imagine the Air Force evolving naturally into a transitional "air and space force," a more fully developed "space and air force" seems counterintuitive—almost analogous to the tail wagging the dog.[88]

Perhaps, the true value of *Global Engagement* was more in the process rather than the product.[89] By being personally involved in the development of these documents and insisting that all the major commands' senior leadership show the same commitment, Fogelman created a process that allowed Air Force senior leadership from all the various fiefdoms within the service to come together and collectively decide on the services' future.[90] Indeed, Fogelman himself thought so. In congressional testimony in 1997, he remarked,

> It was an exciting and fascinating process. Even if we had never produced a document, the intellectual effort would have been worthwhile for the US Air Force. Most importantly, the long-range planning effort left us superbly prepared and finely focused as we entered the QDR. We used the ideas generated by our long-range planning to prepare for the QDR. We will use those same ideas to fulfill our responsibilities in the future.[91]

This is an important and often overlooked point about the role of these strategic plans. Even if these plans do not produce wholesale transformation, there is virtue in the planning process and having the entire senior leadership—from the Chief of Staff and Service Secretary down— discuss the purpose and direction of the service. If nothing else, the process ensures that the disparate parts of the service have a chance to flesh out their differences and ideally agree on a vision of the future. And perhaps this process—even more than *Global Engagement* itself—is Fogelman's legacy to the service.

---

[86] James M. Smith, "Air Force Culture and Cohesion: Building an Air and Space Force for the Twenty-First Century," *Airpower Journal*, Fall 1998.

[87] Benjamin S. Lambeth, *Mastering the Ultimate High Ground: Next Steps in the Military Uses of Space*, Santa Monica, Calif.: RAND Corporation, MR-1649-AF, 2003, p. 2.

[88] Lambeth, 2003, p. 166.

[89] Campbell, 2002, p. 448.

[90] Interview with senior former Air Force strategist, March 2, 2016.

[91] Ronald R. Fogleman, "Statement for General Ronald R. Fogleman Chief of Staff, U.S. Air Force," 1997.

Long-Range Plan (1997)

The following year, the Air Force produced a successor document—the *Long-Range Plan.* Unlike *Global Reach—Global Power* or *Global Engagement,* the *Long-Range Plan* was not a vision document unto itself, but rather, it aimed at "identify[ing] those initial steps and transition decisions which are necessary to reach the goals" in *Global Engagement.*[92] As Fogleman described,

> It is the road map—the architectural framework—for where we go in the future. The second product is a no-kidding, long-range plan that contains objectives and milestones and serves as the actionable part of this process.[93]

Although the *Long-Range Plan* was classified, the Air Force produced an unclassified summary version "to encourage dialogue with industry, think tanks, academia and the public at large on the means to attain these goals."[94] The summary comprised three parts—describing "the 2000–2025 planning context," "sustaining the Air Force core competencies," and then, in the heart of the document, "directive statements."[95] In the latter section, each of the basic issues agreed to at the 1996 Corona conference were broken down by assumptions and constraints; a desired end state; "representative actions" (i.e., a generic set of tasks to accomplish the end state); and, perhaps most importantly, an "office of primary responsibility" responsible for overseeing each task.[96]

By the "directed statements," the Air Force turned fairly vague guidance into concrete tasks. Even the unclassified summary version contains fairly specific guidance for everything from developing and fielding high-altitude UAVs to revamping career progression and professional education.[97] More importantly, perhaps, the *Long-Range Plan* began to shift resources around and turn abstract decisions into fiscal reality. Fogleman understood that strategy and budgeting formed a symbiotic relationship: Strategy needed to affect budgets to produce concrete changes on the service, and the budgeting required a strategy to guide it. For its part, the *Long-Range Plan* reallocated some $2 billion starting in FY 1998, increasing to $8.3 billion in FY 2003. And, in keeping with *Global Engagement*'s focus on space, about 60 percent of these resources were earmarked for "future space operations."[98]

---

[92] Clark A. Murdock, "The Search for a Systemic Solution: Air Force Planning Since the Persian Gulf War," working paper, 2002, p. 11.

[93] Fogleman, 1997.

[94] U.S. Air Force, *The 1997 Air Force Long-Range Plan: Summary*, Washington, D.C., 1997, p. 1.

[95] U.S. Air Force, 1997, p. 2.

[96] U.S. Air Force, 1997.

[97] U.S. Air Force, 1997, pp. 9, 13. For an analysis of Fogleman's role in driving UAV development, see Caitlin Lee, *The Culture of U.S. Air Force Innovation: A Historical Case Study of the Predator Program*, doctoral dissertation, London: Kings College, 2016, pp. 147–183.

[98] Murdock, 2002, p. 17.

Ultimately, the *Long-Range Plan*'s success was more ambiguous than *Global Engagement*. On a budget front, the *Long-Range Plan* struggled to find offsets or cost savings for all its new investments. Originally, Fogleman planned to pay for *Global Engagement* by "divesting" or retiring older systems, but the planners were bogged down about which systems should be retired. In the end, the Air Force decided to shed 35,000 personnel of end strength to pay for modernization, but that was still insufficient.[99] Indeed, according to some observers, the implementation of *Global Engagement* and the *Long-Range Plan* slowed after Fogleman resigned as CSAF in September 1997 in the aftermath of the Khobar Towers terrorist attack. After that, the Air Force turned to other priorities.[100]

America's Air Force Vision 2020 (2000)

Fogleman's successor, Gen Michael Ryan, never intended to coin a new strategy. Indeed, an article in *Air Force Magazine*, written shortly after Ryan took over as CSAF, was titled "The Chief Holds Course."[101] The article quoted Ryan as saying that *Global Engagement* was "an Air Force project, a year and a half in the making, involving all the commands. This was a corporate view of the future. It was not based on individuals."[102] Indeed, Ryan believed that *Global Engagement* was "fundamentally sound" and "a good road map, a good glide path" and argued that "it's now up to us to go out and execute it."[103]

However, several factors changed Ryan's mind. First, the Air Force faced congressional pressure from U.S. Senator Robert Smith to weaponize space and renewed calls for the creation of a separate space force.[104] Second, and perhaps more importantly, in 1999, an American-led North Atlantic Treaty Organization coalition intervened in Kosovo to protect ethnic Albanians from Serbian aggression. Although a comparatively small operation, the Kosovo Air Campaign disproportionally influenced strategy: "Kosovo seemed to validate the Air Force's capacity to halt aggression without waiting for the Army to marshal its divisions and engage."[105] Third, deployments to the Balkans, policing the no-fly zones in Iraq, and others missions were taking

---

[99] Murdock, 2002, p. 18.

[100] Tom Bowman, "Air Force Chief Resigns over Disputes '97 Terrorist Bombing Was Source of Division," *Baltimore Sun*, July 29, 1997; and Barzelay and Campbell, 2003, p. 73. In 1996, a terrorist attack killed 19 airmen at Khobar Towers in Saudi Arabia. After the attack, DoD and Congress disputed who was responsible for the incident and for failing to adequately protect the servicemen.

[101] John A. Tirpak, "The Chief Holds Course," *Air Force Magazine*, January 1998.

[102] Tirpak, 1998, p. 37.

[103] Tirpak, 1998, p. 38.

[104] Barzelay and Campbell, 2003, p. 79; interview with a retired senior Air Force general officer, June 2, 2016. See, also, Murdock, 2001, pp. 25–26.

[105] Barzelay and Campbell, 2003, p. 81. For the debate on whether airpower did indeed win the Kosovo campaign, see Daniel L. Byman and Matthew C. Waxman, "Kosovo and the Great Air Power Debate," *International Security*, Vol. 24, No. 4, Spring 2000.

their toll on the service, and the Air Force was facing a retention problem.[106] Fourth, the Air Force faced an ongoing budget draw down, and the Air Force's senior leaders felt like they needed to better justify their force structure and programs to Congress and DoD's senior leadership.[107] Finally, the Air Force became increasingly worried about the growth of potential adversaries' antiaccess and aerial denial capabilities. In the Air Force–run 1999 futures game, the opponent established an air-exclusion zone of more than 500 miles, beyond the range of many Air Force platforms, including the F-22 Raptor and the F-35 Joint Strike Fighter.[108] According to former Fogleman executive officer Col Jim Engle,

> They [the Air Force leaders] made anti-access/standoff warfare an issue for the fall 1999 Corona and pushed it over the hump from an interesting point of debate to a future policy commitment by the Air Force.[109]

Like Fogleman, Ryan made an active effort to gather and incorporate ideas, although perhaps to a lesser degree.[110] In addition to the Corona conferences, Ryan and Secretary of the Air Force F. Whitten Peters also met with the Air Force four stars every six to eight weeks to further flesh out major decisions confronting the service.[111] The new vision statement, however, was further articulated during a 1999 Corona conference, where the generals wrestled with

> striking the balance between theater specific and global reach and shooting versus enabling platforms. The resolution is to remain theater focused but ask for budget expansion for more global power.[112]

This resolution later became the basis for *America's Air Force Vision 2020: Global Reach, Vigilance, and Power.* Finally, Ryan's planning staff also briefed each of the major Air Force commands on the nascent document, incorporating each Air Force four star's input into the final paper, ultimately released in 2000.[113]

As a process, the crafting of *America's Air Force Vision 2020* generally receives lower marks than Fogleman's *Global Engagement.* Some argue that Peters's (in his role as Under Secretary) participation in the long-term strategy group had a "chilling" effect on discussion.[114] Others blame Ryan. According to Colin Campbell, some participants in the Corona conference

---

[106] Interview with an Air Force senior leader, May 9, 2016; interview with a retired senior Air Force general officer, June 2, 2016.

[107] Interview with a retired senior Air Force general officer, June 2, 2016.

[108] Barzelay and Campbell, 2003, p. 81.

[109] Barzelay and Campbell, 2003, p. 206.

[110] Interview with a former Air Force general officer, June 27, 2016.

[111] Interview with an Air Force senior leader, May 9, 2016.

[112] Barzelay and Campbell, 2003, p. 92.

[113] Interview with a retired senior Air Force general officer, April 27, 2016.

[114] Barzelay and Campbell, 2003, p. 86.

dismissed Ryan as "not visionary, not a strategist."[115] Still others suggest that *America's Air Force Vision 2020* was never intended to be a particularly revolutionary document, but rather a public-relations one—helping to explain to the rank and file, as well as to Capitol Hill, the shift to a rotational force.[116] Either way, *America's Air Force Vision 2020* was not considered to be particularly path-breaking document compared with its predecessors.

As a document, *America's Air Force Vision 2020* adopted a high-level look with few specifics. Clark Murdock argues that it was "mostly an exploration of the identity of the Air Force," rather than a concrete planning document.[117] With a striking picture of the earth on its cover, approximately one-third of the pages are dedicated to photomontages of airmen and aircraft. Much of the text dedicates the Air Force to longstanding, if rather bland, objectives, such as "providing seamless aerospace power," "recruit[ing], train[ing] and maintain[ing] America's best young men and women," and "integrating air, space, and information operations, while leveraging the strengths of each."[118] It, however, successfully quelled some of the discontent left from the *Global Engagement*'s seeming prioritization of space power at the expense of airpower. *America's Air Force Vision 2020* focused on "the blending of air and space capabilities and personnel to advance aerospace power, regardless of where the platforms are located or which ones are chosen."[119]

Ryan championed the Aerospace Expeditionary Force, and its concepts feature prominently in *America's Air Force Vision 2020*.[120] The concept's historical roots lay in the composite air strike task force first proposed after the Korean War.[121] In 1994, under Fogleman's direction, the then–Central Command Air Force commander Lt Gen John Jumper developed the modern incarnation of the concept to enable the Air Force to rapidly deploy to the theater as a response to Iraqi aggression.[122] The concept proposed building self-contained force packages, called *Aerospace Expeditionary Forces*, that could deploy to theater and conduct independent operations relatively quickly.[123] In *America's Air Force Vision 2020*, Ryan took Jumper's idea and expanded the concept and applied it throughout the Air Force.[124] The strategy called for the

---

[115] Campbell, 2002, p. 445.

[116] Interview with an Air Force senior leader, May 9, 2016.

[117] Murdock, 2001, p. 24.

[118] U.S. Air Force, *America's Air Force Vision 2020: Global Reach, Vigilance, and Power*, 2000.

[119] Hays and Mueller, 2001, p. 35.

[120] Barzelay and Campbell, 2003, p. 80.

[121] William L. Dowdy, *Testing the Aerospace Expeditionary Force Concept: An Analysis of AEFs I–IV (1995–97) and the Way Ahead*, Maxwell Air Force Base, Ala.: College of Aerospace Doctrine, Research and Education, Air University, Research Paper 2000-01, 2000, pp. 1, 3.

[122] Dowdy, 2000, pp. 1, 3.

[123] Dowdy, 2000; and interview with a retired senior Air Force general officer, October 11, 2016.

[124] Dowdy, 2000, p. 3; and interview with a retired senior Air Force general officer, June 2, 2016. Critics argue that the Aerospace Expeditionary Force proved overly focused on deploying forces, and, consequently, it failed to

Air Force to be able to form up to ten Aerospace Expeditionary Forces, a deployable Air Force unit capable of providing command and control, intelligence support, air superiority, and strike force for an area about half the size of Texas. The concept was for one Aerospace Expeditionary Force to be always ready to deploy within 48 hours, while another four would be ready to go within 15 days.[125]

The move to Aerospace Expeditionary Forces held the promise for other benefits besides making the force more rapidly responsive. The Aerospace Expeditionary Forces offered the potential to be to the Air Force what carrier strike groups are to the Navy—a relatively simple construct to help Congress and the broader defense community understand its force structure. It also promised to help reduce the strain on the force by shifting to a rotational construct. Given that only one Aerospace Expeditionary Force would be on a short string for a deployment at any given time, the rest of the force could be in a reset phase. The idea was that, by making deployments more predictable for airmen's families, it would increase the service's retention numbers.[126]

Perhaps *America's Air Force Vision 2020*'s most memorable line is the title. Ryan explained it in a joint statement to the House Armed Services Committee on July 11, 2001, with the newly confirmed Secretary of the Air Force James G. Roche:

> Across this spectrum, it was *Global Vigilance, Reach, and Power* that was essential for assuring U.S. national security and international stability. We provided global vigilance using our intelligence, surveillance, and reconnaissance (ISR) assets; force protection measures; and deterrence missions. Our mobility assets and pre-positioned munitions contributed to our global reach. Finally, we displayed global power in Iraq and the Balkans with our unmatched capability to create precise military effects when called upon or threatened. These three facets of aerospace power are interdependent, collectively providing rapid aerospace dominance for America. Perhaps most importantly, all these accomplishments were against the backdrop of a pivotal transformation in the way we structure our forces to support expeditionary operations.[127]

In essence, Ryan argued that vigilance, reach, and power captured the Air Force's core competencies—rapid global mobility, precision engagement, global attack, air and space superiority, information superiority, and agile combat support—and the range of Air Force missions.

---

adequately address the supporting infrastructure requirements. Consequently, it never lived up to its expectations (interview with a former Air Force general officer, June 27, 2016).

[125] U.S. Air Force, 2000.

[126] Interview with an Air Force senior leader, May 9, 2016; and interview with a retired senior Air Force general officer, June 2, 2016.

[127] James G. Roche and Michael E. Ryan, "Joint Statement of the Honorable James G. Roche Secretary of the Air Force and General Michael E. Ryan, Chief of Staff, United States Air Force," July 11, 2001.

"Rapid Aerospace Dominance" (2001)

Not all strategic documents developed made it to publication, but understanding the process behind their development—and why they stalled—can prove equally valuable. "Rapid Aerospace Dominance" provides one such example. After the development of *America's Air Force Vision 2020*, the Air Staff's strategic planning arm, under Maj Gen John Barry, set to work on a strategic concept: rapid aerospace dominance. The concept was designed to link the broader vision of the Air Force expressed in *America's Air Force Vision 2020* with more operational documents to explain "why" the Air Force operates in the way it does.[128] In a nutshell, the concept argued that the Air Force aimed to be able to quickly dominate both *in* the air and space domains and *from* air and space domains to effect surface operations.[129] Beyond simply providing the Air Force with added intellectual coherence, the "Rapid Aerospace Dominance" concept aimed to provide the service a way of explaining Air Force operations to Capitol Hill and the broader policy audience.[130]

Inside the Air Force, the term *rapid aerospace dominance* began to catch on. *Air Force Magazine* noted that the term encompassed "popular themes of future military planning" and called it "seductive and empirical" and "a perfect fit with strategic airpower."[131] And there were plans for a much larger public rollout. By August 2001, the Air Staff produced a series of "Rapid Aerospace Dominance" products—including a draft pamphlet, a draft article intended for *Foreign Affairs* (designed to influence the wider policy audience), an article for *Aerospace Power Journal* (designed to reach more of an Air Force internal audience), and a briefing of more than 80 slides for Air Force senior leaders.[132] Unfortunately, by the time these documents were produced, Ryan's tenure was coming to a close. Ryan tasked the Air Staff to get input from the other Air Force four-star general officers—most importantly, his successor Gen John Jumper, then the commander of Air Combat Command.[133]

Jumper, however, chose not to pursue "Rapid Aerospace Dominance" further. Several possible explanations are given for why that was the case. The new concept came just at the start of a new administration, with the new Secretary of Defense Donald Rumsfeld making a push to transform the department and the military. According to some accounts, Jumper was focused on the Air Force's inputs to the DoD-wide QDR going on simultaneously with "Rapid Aerospace

---

[128] John Barry, "Rapid Aerospace Dominance: A Unifying Concept for the Air Force," unpublished briefing, July 2001.

[129] Barry, 2001.

[130] Interview with a retired Air Force general officer, May 5, 2016.

[131] Rebecca Grant, "The Redefinition of Strategic Airpower," *Air Force Magazine*, October 2003.

[132] Draft copies provided to authors.

[133] Interview with a retired Air Force general officer, May 5, 2016.

Dominance."[134] There also may have been concerns about whether the message—which called for the Air Force dominating the surface (the realm of the Army and Navy) from the air—would cause friction with the other services rather than encourage more joint solutions.[135] Finally, "Rapid Aerospace Dominance" suffered from poor timing. Within days of Jumper taking the helm as CSAF, the September 11 terrorist attacks occurred, and the Air Force's focus turned to Afghanistan and the War on Terrorism.[136] Whatever the reasons, however, without the backing of the Air Force's senior leadership, the strategic concept never took flight, and "Rapid Aerospace Dominance" was never published.

Air Force Transformation Flight Plan (2002, 2003, and 2004)

Secretary of the Air Force Roche and CSAF General Jumper's tenures at the helm of the Air Force were marked by comparatively fewer public strategy documents than in other periods. In the aftermath of the September 11 attacks, the Air Force's focus turned to supporting the Afghanistan and Iraq Wars, rather than producing public documents.[137] This outlook, however, also fit with the Air Force senior leadership's overall approach to strategy at the time. From their standpoint, strategy should start with a concept of operations—how the Air Force would fight in the joint environment—and programs and budgets should flow from that, not with grand theories about airpower or, worse yet, simply replacing old systems with newer ones, without any attention to how these systems would be employed on the battlefield.[138]

One of few public Air Force strategic documents published during this period came in November 2003, when the Air Force released the *U.S. Air Force Transformation Flight Plan*. Signed by Roche and Jumper and spanning 87 pages with almost the same number of pages worth of annexes, the report presented the Air Force's intended transformation efforts over the next several decades.[139] The report was both programmatic and strategic—laying out what equipment the Air Force would buy and implicitly how the service would fight future wars. In a sense, the plan reflected the Air Force senior leadership's thinking at the time, which was that the Air Force did not simply need to prepare to fight the wars taking place at present, but ones

---

[134] Interview with a retired Air Force general officer, May 5, 2016.

[135] Interview with a retired Air Force general officer, April 27, 2016; and interview with a retired senior Air Force general officer, October 11, 2016.

[136] Interview with a senior Air Force leader, April 21, 2016; and interview with a retired senior Air Force general officer, October 11, 2016.

[137] Interview with a retired senior Air Force general officer, October 11, 2016.

[138] Interview with a retired senior Air Force general officer, October 11, 2016.

[139] Headquarters, U.S. Air Force/Future Concepts and Transformation Division, *The U.S. Air Force Transformation Flight Plan*, November 2003, p. i

decades out.[140] Despite the difficulties of projecting that far ahead, planning for the future allowed the Air Force an opportunity to help shape it.[141]

U.S. Air Force Transformation Flight Plan was never intended as a strategy, but rather as an internal reporting document.[142] Then–Secretary of Defense Rumsfeld, an advocate of the revolution in military affairs, believed the services and DoD more broadly were mired in the status quo and needed to change. He therefore pushed the services to detail how they were pursuing transformation. The Air Force dutifully submitted the initial Transformation Flight Plan to the Office of Force Transformation in June 2002, detailing the ways it was trying to evolve.[143] At least as perceived by some on the Air Staff, the initial report proved remarkably successful: Rather than Rumsfeld pressuring the Air Force about the service's perceived rigidity, the Air Force became one of the poster children of transformation. [144]

The Air Force chose to publicly release an updated version of the report in November 2003. Since "Rapid Aerospace Dominance" was never published, the Air Force faced a perceived strategic-messaging void.[145] The Air Force felt it needed a way to publicly explain where it was headed in the future. *The U.S. Air Force Transformation Flight Plan* also was an attempt to explain the Air Force's new approach to strategy, in which a distinct concept of operations detailing how the Air Force would respond to future needs was part of the joint force that would drive the Air Force's planning and programming.[146] And so, almost accidentally, what originally was an internal reporting document became a strategic plan.

The U.S. Air Force Transformation Flight Plan's scope was remarkably broad. It included chapters on reforming everything from the Air Force's culture to its business processes. The part of the report that attracted the most attention, however, was Chapter Seven, "Developing Transformational Capabilities," detailing the Air Force's research and development and procurement priorities in the near (until 2010), middle, and long terms (post-2015). Most of the programs were fairly traditional, such as the Global Hawk long-range remotely piloted vehicle, F-35 Joint Strike Fighter, and the next-generation bomber.[147] A handful of the proposals for longer-term development, however, were more cutting edge. The report called for research on "hypervelocity rod bundles" (heavy metal [e.g., tungsten] rods placed in space that could be

---

[140] Interview with a senior Air Force leader, April 21, 2016.

[141] Interview with a senior Air Force leader, April 21, 2016.

[142] Interview with an Air Force action officer, September 13, 2016.

[143] Headquarters, U.S. Air Force/Future Concepts and Transformation Division, 2003, p. i

[144] Interview with an Air Force action officer, September 13, 2016.

[145] Interview with an Air Force action officer, September 13, 2016.

[146] Headquarters, U.S. Air Force/Future Concepts and Transformation, 2003, pp. v–vii; and interview with a retired senior Air Force general officer, October 11, 2016.

[147] Headquarters, U.S. Air Force/Future Concepts and Transformation, 2003, pp. 55, 66.

dropped on an adversary) and "Evolutionary Air and Space Global Laser Engagement (EAGLE) Airship Relay Mirrors," to name two.[148]

Perhaps because it was originally intended to report current efforts at transformation rather than necessarily drive new initiatives, the white paper did not appear to have a significant effect on the debates about Air Force transformation. The *Flight Plan* received glancing mentions in a handful of academic and think-tank works, which primarily discussed the technical and policy implications of missile defense and long-range strike.[149] There is also little evidence that the *Flight Plan* translated into budgetary gains for the service. Indeed, both the Brookings Institution and Federation of American Scientists came out with papers advocating to cancel many of the more futuristic Air Force proposals—particularly the offensive space weapons (i.e., the lasers and the hypervelocity rod bundles)—in favor of cheaper alternatives.[150]

In the popular press, the *Flight Plan* was a public-relations debacle. NBC News labeled it as a "futuristic flight plan" that "plans for a future war in space."[151] The *New York Times* raised questions about the costs and practicality of some of the concepts.[152] The *Atlanta Journal-Constitution* argued the technologies listed in the *Flight Plan*—such as EAGLE—were horribly misaligned for U.S. strategic needs, namely winning the war on terrorism.[153] ABC News noted widespread opposition to the plan, from arms-control advocates both within the United States and among European allies.[154] The *Flight Plan* even attracted attention on the other side of the globe. The *New Zealand Herald* ran editorials arguing that the *Flight Plan*'s proposal defied physics and jeopardized arms control.[155] If part of the purpose of strategic documents is to help favorably shape public opinion both in the United States and abroad, the *Flight Plan* clearly struggled.

---

[148] Headquarters, U.S. Air Force/Future Concepts and Transformation, 2003, pp. 65–66.

[149] See, for example, Michael Krepon, "A Case Study in Policy Entrepreneurship," Washington, D.C.: The Stimson Center, undated, p. 8; Barry D. Watts, *Long-Range Strike: Imperatives, Urgency and Options*, Washington, D.C.: Center for Strategic and Budgetary Assessments, April 2005, p. 73; and Bruce M. Sugden, "Speed Kills: Analyzing the Deployment of Conventional Ballistic Missiles," *International Security*, Vol. 34, No. 1, Summer 2009, p. 114.

[150] Deborah Shapley, "Space: FAS Redefines the Threat," *Journal of the Federation of American Scientists*, Vol. 57, No. 4, Fall 2004; and Jeffrey M. Tebbs, "Pruning the Defense Budget," Washington, D.C.: The Brookings Institution, January 2007.

[151] Leonard David, "Air Force Plans for Future War in Space," NBC News, February 23, 2004.

[152] Jonathan Shainin, "Rods from God," *New York Times Magazine*, December 10, 2006.

[153] In a biting editorial, Jay Bookman, deputy editorial page editor of the *Atlanta Journal-Constitution*, quipped,

> So we are going to shoot this laser up into space, bounce it off this perfectly positioned mirror, and them aim the beam down into Baghdad to evaporate Abu Musab al Zarqawi? This is madness. As [counterinsurgency author Robert] Taber might put it, we cannot win the war of the flea by building a bigger, more powerful and expensive purebred dog. (Jay Bookman, "U.S. Planning for the War It Wishes For," *Atlanta Journal-Constitution*, May 19, 2005, p. 19A)

[154] Marc Lallanilla, "Shooting Stars," ABC News, March 30, 2004.

[155] Peter Huck, "The Race of the Space Warriors," *New Zealand Herald*, September 22, 2006.

In 2004, the Air Force released a new *Transformation Flight Plan*. This version made a conscious effort to tone down the earlier version's futuristic voice.[156] It did not include any reference to hypervelocity rod bundles and only a passing mention of airborne lasers.[157] By 2005, the series was discontinued altogether. As the Iraq and Afghanistan Wars heated up, Rumsfeld's push toward transformation began to falter. The Air Force still provided the data contained in *Transformation Flight Plan* to Rumsfeld—just in an internal publication.[158] Moreover, the Air Force had a new CSAF, Gen T. Michael Moseley, who wanted to publish his own vision for the Air Force's future, so a *Transformation Flight Plan* did not need to fill the public space.

Ultimately, the fallout from the 2003 *Transformation Flight Plan* highlights the importance of judging the environment and challenges of tailoring the audience with strategic documents. To the public, with the United States struggling to fight counterinsurgencies in Iraq and Afghanistan, these futuristic proposals that might defeat technologically sophisticated nation-states seemed ill timed, if not tone deaf. In the *Transformation Flight Plan*'s defense, it provided Rumsfeld and the Office of the Secretary of Defense what they wanted—a long-term plan, not a short-term fix, to current battles. Moreover, the outcry ignored some very real changes the Air Force was making to improve its performance in the current wars, such as revamping Air Force special operations training or refining the airlift system to speed the transportation of supplies to troops in theater.[159] And many of the technologies listed in the *Transformation Flight Plan*—including Global Hawk, the F-35, and the long-range bomber—are becoming realties. Still, the outcry over the 2003 *Transformation Flight Plan* underscores how successful internal documents may not necessarily make for successful external ones.

Lasting Heritage . . . Limitless Horizons: A Warfighter's Vision (2006)

In fall 2005, Gen T. Michael Moseley became the new CSAF, and Michael Wynne became the Air Force Secretary. Shortly thereafter, on February 28, 2006, the Air Force got a new vision as well—*Lasting Heritage . . . Limitless Horizon: A Warfighter's Vision*. This document was designed to replace the *America's Air Force Vision 2020: Global Reach, Vigilance, and Power* released several years earlier.[160] According to Moseley, the vision stressed three priorities: fighting the global war on terrorism, developing airmen, and modernizing the force.[161] The glossy, photo-filled 25-page document was nearly twice as long as *Vision 2020*, but this was

---

[156] Interview with an Air Force action officer, September 13, 2016.

[157] Headquarters, U.S. Air Force/Future Concepts and Transformation Division, *The U.S. Air Force Transformation Flight Plan*, 2004.

[158] Interview with an Air Force action officer, September 13, 2016.

[159] Interview with an Air Force senior leader, April 22, 2016.

[160] Julie Weckerlein, "Air Force Vision Embraces Warfighters, Heritage," *Air Force Print News*, February 28, 2006.

[161] Weckerlein, 2006.

mostly devoted to a timeline of the major Air Force milestones and quotes from senior Air Force leaders past and present. In the last couple pages, *Lasting Heritage* gave concrete objectives for the Air Force's direction for the next 15 years, including increasing its number of command, control, communications, computers, intelligence, surveillance, and reconnaissance platforms by 70 percent; increasing the number of special operations and combat search and rescue platforms by 88 percent; and reducing the number of fighter aircraft by 25 percent.[162] It also included relatively clear goals, ranging from providing trained and ready airmen to increasing the Air Force's audit readiness.[163] As is often the case, *Lasting Heritage* was accompanied by a press release but seems to have attracted little additional attention.[164] That said, the resource shifts that *Lasting Heritage* predicted ultimately occurred, thanks partially to the next strategic document: the *Air Force Roadmap 2006–2025*.

Air Force Roadmap (2006, 2008)

A few months later, in June 2006, the Air Force published *Air Force Roadmap 2006–2025*, a glossy 159-page monograph. The document's stated purpose was "a capability-based force structure plan that conveys the planned recapitalization and modernization of the Air Force through 2025."[165] The *Roadmap* tried to translate the DoD-wide 2006 QDR into programmatic details for the service.[166] Specifically, it charted out how many of the older major Air Force platforms—from aircraft to satellites—would gradually be phased out and what platforms would take their place.

Like the 2003 *Transformation Flight Plan,* the *Roadmap* aimed at transformation but was less radical in its scope. Unlike the *Transformation Flight Plan*, there is no explicit mention of the much-derided "hypervelocity rod bundles" or the EAGLE system in the 2006 document. In fact, the *Roadmap* limits itself to a couple of anodyne references to laser weapons altogether, noting that "[t]he Air Force is investing significant resources in directed energy technology, to include lasers and high powered microwaves" and that "directed energy weapons will allow truly surgical precision, including a variety of non-lethal effects."[167] The Air Force, thereby, avoided much of the popular ridicule that accompanied the 2003 *Transformation Flight Plan*. At the same time, the *Roadmap* failed to generate much positive press.

On January 16, 2008, CSAF General Moseley released a new version of the *U.S. Air Force Roadmap.* Like its predecessor, the *Roadmap* aimed at "recapitalization and modernization of its

---

[162] U.S. Air Force, *Lasting Heritage . . . Limitless Horizons: A Warfighter's Vision*, February 2006a, p. 23.

[163] U.S. Air Force 2006a, p. 24.

[164] Weckerlein, 2006.

[165] U.S. Air Force, *Air Force Roadmap 2006–2025*, June 2006b, p 6.

[166] U.S. Air Force, 2006b, p. 10.

[167] U.S. Air Force, 2006b, p. 137.

aging Air Force fleet" and outlined priorities for next-generation aircraft, including the next-generation bomber, tanker, and F-35 Joint Strike Fighter.[168] This version, however, had one key new addition. Organized under General Ryan's grouping of global vigilance, global reach, and global power, the report outlined where in the United States these future aircraft would likely be homebased.[169] Although *Wired* referred to the *Roadmap* as the "big map tease," the report may have another, more political purpose in mind.[170] The Air Force Association noted,

> Although senior Air Force leaders won't say so in so many words, the service's new beddown roadmap is a map of constituencies and effectively puts members of Congress on notice that if they want an Air Force mission in their district, they better support the buying of the new systems. If they don't, and inventories continue to shrink, the missions—and the bases, and Air National Guard and Air Force Reserve Command units associated with them—will surely go away.[171]

And in this respect, although the *Roadmap* did not break new strategic ground, it accomplished a more political purpose. Several local newspapers noticed what aircraft might be stationed at their local airbases.[172] The influential think tank *Council on Foreign Relations* included a link to the *Roadmap* on its website.[173] More importantly, perhaps, influential U.S. Senator John Thune praised the *Roadmap* for identifying South Dakota's Ellsworth Air Force Base as a potential home for the long-range bomber and Joe Foss Field as a potential base for the F-35 Joint Strike Fighter. He stated,

> Today's report indicates that South Dakota remains an integral part of our national security system. Our people, our communities, our unique geographical location and our commitment to the troops and their missions continue to make South Dakota an ideal location to base and house some of America's top military assets.[174]

Senator Thune later emphasized his praise for the report when Wynne and Moseley testified before the Senate Armed Services Committee in March 2008.[175] If the *Roadmap* wanted to

---

[168] U.S. Air Force, "Air Force Chief of Staff Releases Future Roadmap," Washington, D.C., Release No. 040108, January 16, 2008.

[169] U.S. Air Force, 2008.

[170] David Axe, "Air Force's Big 'Roadmap' Tease," *Wired*, January 17, 2008a.

[171] Axe, 2008a.

[172] See, for example, Sue Major Holmes, "Three N.M. Bases Getting New Planes Under USAF 'Road Map,'" Associated Press, January 16, 2008; Ted Jackovics, "MacDill in the Running for New Flying Tankers," *Tampa Tribune*, February 15, 2008; and "Cannon Addresses 'Air Force Roadmap,'" *Clovis News Journal*, January 16, 2008.

[173] Council on Foreign Relations, "Air Force Weapon System Roadmap," January 16, 2008.

[174] John Thune, "Senator Thune Hails Air Force Report," U.S. Senator for South Dakota John Thune website, January 14, 2008.

[175] "Transcript on Armed Services Committee Hearing on the Air Force Tanker Competition," U.S. Senator for Alabama Jeff Sessions website, March 5, 2008.

generate political support for Air Force procurement, it clearly notched a small but important win.

The Nation's Guardians (2007)

Moseley also penned a CSAF white paper, *The Nation's Guardians: America's 21st-Century Air Force*. It proclaimed,

> Ascendant powers—flush with new wealth and hungry for resources and status—are posturing to contest U.S. superiority. These adaptive competitors are translating lessons from recent conflicts into new warfighting concepts, capabilities and doctrines specifically designed to counter U.S. strengths and exploit vulnerabilities.[176]

The white paper cited as evidence gains by other unnamed nations in "fourth generation plus" fighter aircraft, expansion in potential adversaries' integrated air defenses, and the proliferation of unmanned aerial systems.[177] It argued that the Air Force "has been in continuous combat since 1990—17 years and counting—taking a toll on our people and rapidly aging equipment" and advocated robust programs to modernize the force.[178]

Despite a mere ten pages and considerably less flashy than other Air Force strategy documents, *The Nation's Guardians* attracted popular attention for its focus on ascendant powers.[179] While the statements seem innocuous enough, the press portrayed the white paper as a call for the Air Force to focus more on conventional threats from Russia and China, rather than Secretary of Defense Robert Gates's focus on unconventional warfare.[180] To add to the controversy, the statements occurred also in the midst of a budget battle over purchase of the F-22 Raptor—the sophisticated air superiority fighter that many in the Air Force favored as a hedge against Russia and China, but which Gates felt was ill suited to wars at hand.[181] After all, he noted, "we had been at war for ten years, and the plane had not flown a single combat mission."[182] For his part, Moseley claims he never intended to contradict Secretary Gates. Rather, he wanted to push back on the "interesting assumption in the world of Washington right now that the dominating piece of the air domain, air superiority, is somehow a given, is

---

[176] T. Michael Moseley, *The Nation's Guardians: America's 21st-Century Air Force*, Chief of Staff, U.S. Air Force white paper, December 29, 2007, p. 4.

[177] Moseley, 2007, p. 4.

[178] Moseley, 2007, p. 7.

[179] David Axe, "Army Strategy Manual Gets It Right," *Wired*, February 27, 2008b.

[180] Peter Spiegel, "Air Force Outlines Strategic Plan: Conventional and Newer Types of Threats Are Both Accounted For," *Los Angeles Times*, February 8, 2008.

[181] Robert Gates, *Duty: Memoirs of a Secretary at War*, New York: Alfred A. Knopf, 2014, pp. 318–319.

[182] Gates, 2014, p. 319.

somehow a birthright" and stress the need to prepare the Air Force for the full spectrum of conflict.[183]

As it turns out, Moseley never fully implemented the new vision. Only four months after unveiling the new plan, Secretary Gates asked for Moseley and Secretary of the Air Force Michael Wynne's resignations after the Air Force was rocked by a series of controversies, including a B-52 bomber accidentally flying six live nuclear warheads across the country, nuclear fuzes accidentally being shipped to Taiwan, and the awarding of a dubious $50 million contract to a former senior general officer.[184]

2008 *Air Force Strategic Plan* (October Version)/*CSAF Vectors 2010* and *2011*

Unlike his predecessors, Moseley's successor as CSAF, Gen Norton Schwartz, was neither a fighter nor a bomber pilot, but rather a mobility pilot who spent much of his career in special operations.[185] Coming in after the departure of Wynne and Moseley, he was—according to some observers—tasked with "stopping the bleeding" and steadying a service in turmoil, rather than rocking the boat with new ideas.[186] The task suited his temperament. Skeptical of the utility of long-planning monographs, Schwartz preferred shorter statements issued on a regular basis. Schwartz, along with the new Secretary of the Air Force Michael Donley, released a new version of the *Air Force Strategic Plan* in 2008. Designed for internal consumption, it struck a different, more minimalist and substantive tone. It did not feature photomontages and, aside from a handful of tables and a flowchart, had few visuals. It emphasized five priorities—strengthening the nuclear enterprise, partnering with the joint and coalition team in operations, caring for airmen and their families, modernization, and acquisition reform—with subordinate concrete goals underneath each heading. Importantly, it also included tasks to the Air Staff on how to execute the new strategy.[187]

Schwartz's *CSAF Vector*, however, probably best captured his approach to strategy. Schwartz was not the first CSAF to issue *CSAF Vector* to the force. Ryan issued periodic "Notes to Airmen." Similarly, Moseley, Schwartz's immediate predecessor, issued *CSAF Vector* periodically during his tenure as well, but these messages typically addressed specific issues. For example, one issued in January 2006 addressed "Advanced Composite Wing Training," and

---

[183] Spiegel, 2008.

[184] Thom Shanker, "2 Top Leaders of Air Force Pushed Out After Inquiry," *New York Times*, June 6, 2008; Gates, 2014, pp. 239–245.

[185] U.S. Air Force, "General Norton A. Schwartz," August 2012.

[186] Interview with a retired senior Air Force general officer, May 11, 2016; and interview with retired Air Force general officer, June 27, 2016.

[187] Norton A. Schwartz and Michael B. Donley, *2008 Air Force Strategic Plan*, Washington, D.C.: Department of the Air Force, October 2008.

another issued in September 2007 addressed "discipline" in the force.[188] Unlike Moseley, Schwartz adopted the vector format to set out his vision and strategy for the Air Force as whole.

Schwartz's *CSAF Vectors* also broke from previous strategic documents in several key ways. First, they were short. The 2010 *CSAF Vector* ran only seven pages long; the 2011 *CSAF Vector* was eight pages. In stark contrast to the overall trend in strategic documents, the *CSAF Vector* texts simply comprised words: no photographs of airplanes or smiling airmen, no graphs, and no visuals of any kind. More subtly, perhaps, the *CSAF Vector* documents also differed in that they were the *CSAF's documents*, rather than an *Air Force* document. The *CSAF Vector* documents were also substantively more focused. The 2010 Vector reinforced the same five major priorities as the October 2008 *Air Force Strategic Plan*, with new concrete tasks underneath each heading.[189] For the most part, the 2011 Vector kept the same format and just updated the subtasks, based on what was accomplished previously.[190] For better or worse, they were General Schwartz's priorities, and although they were coordinated with the civilian leadership, the document bore only Schwartz's (not the Secretary of the Air Force's) signature.[191]

Schwartz signed both the 2010 and 2011 Vectors on July 4 and then publicly rolled out the documents over the following weeks.[192] Apart from the Air Force press release, an article in the *Air Forces Times*, and a cross-post on the popular military analysis blog *Small Wars Journal*, the Vectors attracted little external attention.[193] Inside the Air Force, however, the Vectors garnered more attention. Multiple pieces about the Air Force, penned by Air Force officers, cite the Vectors (although rarely at any length) mostly for their emphasis on building partnership capacity and operating in a joint environment.[194] Internally, the 2011 Vector cites a host of accomplishments—from expanding Joint Terminal Air Controller support to opening a new Deployment Transition Center at Ramstein Air Force Base in Germany to completing the

---

[188] For a content analysis of these and similar messages, see Carolyn Chu, Brandon Dues, and Laura L. Miller, *Cultural Themes in Messages from Top Air Force Leaders, 2005–2008*, Santa Monica, Calif.: RAND Corporation, DB-583-AF, 2010. For press coverage of the vector, see Janie Santos, "Latest 'Vector' Highlights Importance of Discipline," *Air Force News Agency*, September 13, 2007.

[189] Norton A. Schwartz, *CSAF Vector 2010*, July 4, 2010.

[190] Norton A. Schwartz, *CSAF Vector 2011*, July 4, 2011.

[191] Schwartz, 2010, 2011.

[192] See Janie Santos, "CSAF Releases 'Vector,'" *Defense Media Activity-San Antonio*, July 13, 2010.

[193] Scott Fontaine, "Schwartz: Way Ahead Includes Modernization, International Cooperation," *Air Force Times*, July 27, 2010, p. 21.

[194] For example, see Thomas K. Livingston, *Building the Capacity of Partner States Through Security Force Assistance*, Washington, D.C.: Congressional Research Service, R41817, May 5, 2011; Chris Wachter, "Air-Mindedness: The Core of Successful Air Enterprise Development," *Air and Space Power Journal*, January–February 2012; and James H. Drape, "Building Partnership Capacity: Operation Harmattan and Beyond," *Air and Space Power Journal*, September–October 2012.

competition for a new refueling aircraft—all accomplished since the 2010 Vector.[195] How many of these accomplishments would have occurred without the 2010 Vector is debatable. Ultimately, from their observable effect, Schwartz's *CSAF Vector* documents had a modest effect on the force, with little external effect.

The World's Greatest Air Force—Powered by Airmen, Fueled by Innovation (2013)

Schwartz's successor as CSAF, Gen Mark Welsh III, returned to the previous practice of authoring and releasing strategic documents designed to speak to a wider, public audience. The first was *The World's Greatest Air Force—Powered by Airmen, Fueled by Innovation: A Vision for the United States*, released in January 2013. Only three pages in length, half of which were photographs, the vision statement arguably did not break much new ground. As its name implies, *The World's Greatest Air Force* was less a strategy and more a general statement of principles. It recommitted the Air Force to its core missions and to its airmen. It charged that "every Airman should constantly look for smarter ways to do business."[196] Finally, near the end of the document, *The World's Greatest Air Force* alluded to the forthcoming Air Force publication: *Global Vigilance, Global Reach, Global Power for America*.

Global Vigilance, Global Reach, Global Power for America (2013)

About eight months after *The World's Greatest Air Force*, in August 2013, Welsh issued *Global Vigilance, Global Reach, Global Power for America*. The document was started under Schwartz but completed under Welsh.[197] Its name hearkened back to the Ryan, McPeak, and Fogleman strategy documents. At 12 pages, *Global Vigilance, Global Reach, Global Power* was only marginally longer than Schwartz's vectors, but it struck a different tone. It was not intended as a strategy but rather "a more comprehensive presentation of how USAF [U.S. Air Force] core missions (air and space superiority; intelligence, surveillance, and reconnaissance; rapid global mobility; global strike; and command and control) contribute to the defense of the nation."[198] It contains numerous photographs of airmen and aircraft. Its introductory page features a series of tributes by a variety of senior leaders—from Hap Arnold to Winston Churchill to Lyndon

---

[195] Schwartz, 2011, pp. 5, 6, 8. Importantly, some of these initiatives were in the works long before the Vector mentioned them. For example, the funding for the Deployment Transition Center started in the mid-2000s (interview with a retired Air Force general officer, August 10, 2016).

[196] U.S. Air Force, *The World's Greatest Air Force—Powered by Airmen, Fueled by Innovation: A Vision for the United States*, January 2013a.

[197] Correspondence with an Air Force analyst, May 31, 2016.

[198] Vick, 2015, p. 80.

Johnson—to the Air Force and its mission.[199] *Global Vigilance, Global Reach, Global Power* was even accompanied by two-minute promotional YouTube video featuring Welsh introducing the document.[200]

Substantively, *Global Vigilance, Global Reach, Global Power* highlighted similar themes as previous roles and missions. It stressed airpower's importance as a tool of national power and airmen's role in promoting innovation. Like the *Global Presence* (1995), it also contained an expression of the Air Force's own institutional insecurity and continuous need to defend its existence as an independent service:

> The air arms of the Army, Navy, and Marine Corps are supremely capable at what they do—facilitating their parent Service's respective mastery of operations on the ground, at sea, and in a littoral environment. However, America has only one Air Force that was specifically designed and is precisely employed to exploit the unique global advantages realized from operating in air, space, and cyberspace.[201]

Indeed, the *Diplomat*'s review of *Global Vigilance, Global Reach, Global Power* noted, "The document is hardly revolutionary, and to some extent serves as an example of how deep concerns about autonomy and independence continue to animate the Air Force."[202]

Underneath the flash, however, *Global Vigilance, Global Reach, Global Power* contained a serious message. Although it never explicitly mentioned the Air Force's fiscal challenges thanks to the Budget Control Act's sequestration cuts in 2013, it argues that the Air Force provides "a flexible, precise, and lethal force that is capable of rapidly responding anywhere on the globe . . . at a relatively low cost in relation to the return on investment."[203] Importantly, *Global Vigilance, Global Reach, Global Power* concludes with a warning about the Air Force budget:

> Investments in Air Force capabilities and readiness are essential if the Nation is to maintain an agile, flexible, and ready force. To be effective, this force must be deliberately planned for and appropriately and consistently funded. Our highly sophisticated and capable Air Force cannot be reconstituted overnight if it is allowed to atrophy.[204]

Perhaps unsurprisingly then, Assistant Secretary of the Air Force for Acquisition William LaPlante's and the Deputy Chief of Staff for Operations, Plans, and Requirements Lieutenant

---

[199] U.S. Air Force, *Global Vigilance, Global Reach, Global Power for America*, 2013b.

[200] U.S. Air Force, "Global Vigilance, Global Reach, Global Power for America," U.S. Air Force YouTube channel, August 22, 2013c.

[201] U.S. Air Force, 2013b, p. 2.

[202] "The U.S. Air Force's New Game Plan in the Asia-Pacific," *The Diplomat*, October 9, 2013.

[203] U.S. Air Force, 2013b, p. 2.

[204] U.S. Air Force, 2013b, p. 12.

Gen Burton Field used language in *Global Vigilance, Global Reach, Global Power* to frame their congressional testimony on the future of combat aircraft purchases.[205]

Like many of the other documents, assessing the effect of *Global Vigilance, Global Reach, Global Power* proves difficult. Like its predecessors, there are mentions of the document in Air Force public relations press releases.[206] The YouTube introduction to the pamphlet also had more than 17,250 views by January 25, 2016.[207] Whether the document actually ensured that the Air Force is "deliberately planned for and appropriately and consistently funded" is, perhaps, more debatable.[208] Welsh, however, did use the document as a cornerstone of his later congressional testimony about the damage sequestration was doing to the Air Force.[209] Ultimately, the outcry from Welsh—as well as from his fellow service chiefs and the rest of the defense establishment—helped push Congress to pass the Bipartisan Budget Act of 2013, which provided most sequestration relief.[210] In this sense then, *Global Vigilance, Global Reach, Global Power* proved a modest, if indirect, success.

America's Air Force: A Call to the Future (2014)

The next document produced under Welsh's tenure was *America's Air Force: A Call to the Future*, dated July 2014. In his introduction, Welsh explained the logic of how *America's Air Force* fit with the preceding documents:

> Over the last 18 months, we released two foundational documents to help us define the United States Air Force for the twenty-first century. The first, *America's Greatest Air Force—Powered by Airmen, Fueled by Innovation*, describes who we are—an exceptional team of innovative Airmen, grounded in our Core Values, superbly trained and equipped to execute five core missions. The second document, *Global Vigilance, Global Reach, Global Power* explains what we do . . . Building upon "who we are" and "what we do," this *Strategy*

---

[205] William A. LaPlante and Burton M. Field, "Fiscal Year 2015 Combat Aviation Programs," Washington, D.C.: Department of the Air Force Presentation to the House Armed Services Committee Subcommittee on Tactical Air and Land Forces, March 26, 2014.

[206] For example, see Air Force News Service, "AF Leaders Cite Airmen as Bedrock in New Core Mission Document," August 22, 2013a; Air Force News Service, "Every Airman Matters, Each Story Is Important," August 29, 2013b.

[207] U.S. Air Force, 2013c. By way of comparison, the Air Force's end strength—active, reserve, Guard, and civilians—numbered more than 650,000 during the same period of time. Air Force Personnel Center, "Air Force Personnel Demographics," September 30, 2016; and DoD, "Department of Defense (DoD) Releases Fiscal Year 2017 President's Budget Proposal," Washington, D.C., NR-046-16, February 9, 2016.

[208] U.S. Air Force, 2013b, p. 12.

[209] Mark A. Welsh III, "The Strategic Choices and Management Review," Washington, D.C.: Department of the Air Force Presentation to the House Armed Services Committee, September 18, 2013.

[210] Kristina Wong, "Pentagon Welcomes Budget Deal but Wants More Money," *Washington Times*, December 11, 2013.

provides a general path of "where we need to go" to ensure our Air Force meets the needs of our great Nation over the next 30 years.[211]

Ultimately, *America's Air Force* would be one of five documents produced under Welsh's tenure—including *The World's Greatest Air Force*; *Global Vigilance, Global Reach, Global Power*; *Air Force Future Operating Concept: A View of the Air Force in 2035*; and the *Strategic Master Plan*—that aimed at defining a vision for the future and strengthening the Air Force's enduring contributions to national defense.

The tone of *America's Air Force* was different from that of *The World's Greatest Air Force* and *Global Vigilance, Global Reach, Global Power*. Running about 20 pages, it was longer but clearly written and relatively free of jargon, abbreviations, and photomontages. Instead, it touched on a range of policy priorities going forward—from personnel policies (such as the active-reserve spectrum of service and civil service–military relations) to capability development (in terms of ISR and high-end strike capabilities).[212] Finally, *America's Air Force* outlined the service's top research and development priorities—including hypersonics, nanotechnology, directed energy, and unmanned and autonomous systems.[213]

After its release, *America's Air Force* attracted attention outside the Air Force. As with its predecessors, the Air Force issued a press release with its publication.[214] *America's Air Force*, however, also attracted more attention among the policy and defense worlds.[215] Moreover, much of this attention was positive. Sydney Freedberg of the popular defense news service *Breaking Defense* commented:

> The grander the title, the blander the content. That's normally a safe rule in Washington. But if analyzed closely, this afternoon's "State of the Air Force" briefing by service Secretary Deborah Lee James and Chief of Staff Mark Welsh, plus the accompanying pamphlet A Call To the Future, actually do articulate a remarkably clear vision of where the U.S. Air Force wants to be—and where it fears it'll end up instead.[216]

Specifically, Freedberg lauded *America's Air Force* for clearly stating the services' intent to focus on such high-end threats as China.[217] He also noted that *America's Air Force* charted a path forward on acquisition: "Huge, long-term programs limit our options; we are too often left with 'all or nothing' outcomes and 'double or nothing' budget decisions," which subtly reveal a

---

[211] U.S. Air Force, *America's Air Force: A Call to the Future*, July 2014, p. 5.

[212] U.S. Air Force, 2014, pp. 12–13, 15–16.

[213] U.S. Air Force, 2014, p. 19.

[214] Air Force Public Affairs Agency, "Strategic Agility Is the Future of the Air Force," July 30, 2014.

[215] See, for example, Joey Cheng, "Air Force's 30-Year Plan Seeks 'Strategic Agility,'" *Defense Systems*, July 31, 2014.

[216] Sydney J. Freedberg, Jr., "Air Force to Focus on High-Threat Future, If Congress Lets It: James and Welsh," *Breaking Defense*, July 30, 2014.

[217] Freedberg 2014.

reluctance to pursue another large-scale acquisition program, such as the F-35 Joint Strike Fighter.[218]

Whether the Air Force will be able to enact this future remains to be seen. For all its desire to focus on high-end threats, the Air Force lost its battle with Congress to retire the A-10 Warthog—the slow, low-flying tank-killing aircraft used in the fight against the Islamic State—and replace it with the newer stealthy F-35 Joint Strike Fighter.[219] Still, *America's Air Force* at least forced the conversation.

Air Force Future Operating Concept: A View of the Air Force in 2035 (2015)

America's Air Force was followed by the *Air Force Future Operating Concept: A View of the Air Force in 2035*, published in September 2015. It aimed to "provide a picture of future operations that informs Air Force Strategy by describing the desired future state for force development."[220] Perhaps unsurprisingly given its expanded mandate, the *Future Operating Concept* is considerably longer (47 pages) than the three earlier documents produced under Welsh's tenure as chief, but it strikes some similar themes. It focuses on "operational agility" comprising "flexibility, speed, coordination, balance and strength."[221] It underscores the transitional "multidomain operations" wherein cyber, space, and air operations are increasingly integrated.[222] The *Future Operating Concept* differed from its predecessors, however, because it went on not only to describe the future operating concept but also to depict a fictional scenario about how the Air Force could respond—across all domains in an integrated fashion—in 2035.[223]

The *Future Operating Concept* received mixed reviews. Mackenzie Eaglen, a defense analyst at the American Enterprise Institute, hailed it as "new and innovative." In her review of the paper, she wrote,

> In the sixth year of a decade-long defense spending cut, it is immensely refreshing to read Air Force leadership once again unleashed to consider how they plan to dominate the adversary and achieve operational victory over a much tougher enemy than those of the recent past.[224]

Air Force officer and strategist Col Michael Pietrucha, however, took a more pessimistic view. He blasted all the services for "future operating concept hubris," expecting that the United

---

[218] U.S. Air Force, 2014, p. 9; and Freedberg, 2014.

[219] Brendan McGarry, "Congress to Air Force: Push to Retire A-10 'Misguided,'" *DoD Buzz*, September 30, 2015.

[220] U.S. Air Force, 2015, p. 4.

[221] U.S. Air Force, 2015, p. 7.

[222] U.S. Air Force, 2015, p. 8.

[223] U.S. Air Force, 2015.

[224] Mackenzie Eaglen, "Air Force Delivers New and Innovative Vision of Future Warfare," *Real Clear Defense*, September 15, 2015.

States will enjoy decisive superiority over its rivals in 2035.[225] He accused the Air Force in particular of expecting that the complex set of systems will run smoothly in the future:

> It is bitterly ironic that a service that still believes in inflicting strategic paralysis on an enemy should so readily champion a concept that sets its own decision-making processes up for catastrophic failure when the promised information flows are disrupted, distorted, and deceived.[226]

Perhaps more problematically, while the *Future Operating Concept* showed how the future could look two decades down the road, it was less clear on how the Air Force could get there. In a sense, it was largely an aspirational document rather than a practical plan with a clear way ahead. In fairness, this function—bridging the present to the future—fell to its sister document, the *Strategic Master Plan*, released at roughly the same time.

Ultimately, it is too soon to fully evaluate the *Future Operating Concept* and the *Strategic Master Plan*'s effect on the service. Since both were publicly released at the end of 2015, the degree to which these documents will shape the Air Force's budget and structure remain an open question, and these topics will be evaluated elsewhere in other RAND studies.

Conclusions from the Period

In the more than a quarter century since *Global Reach—Global Power*, Air Force strategic documents have certainly become stylistically slicker. They now incorporate more photographs and inspirational quotes and are often rolled out with an accompanying public relations campaign, complete with press releases and YouTube videos. Whether today's documents have become more influential and shaped the Air Force more profoundly than those decades earlier is uncertain.

Collectively, however, these documents produced the same benefits as those from earlier periods of Air Force history. First, some documents—such as the *Long-Range Plan,* the *Transformation Flight Plan*, and the *Air Force Roadmap*—have shaped how the Air Force justified and allocated its resources, defining what technologies the Air Force chooses to develop and what systems it procures. Second, other documents helped shaped the structure of the Air Force. For better or worse, *Blueprints for the Objective Force* left a lasting mark on the structure of the service. Third, and perhaps more importantly, these documents have met the 1989 Air Force paper's challenge and given the Air Force a sense of identity and purpose—separate from the other services. Indeed, that the same series of words—*global reach, global power* (now with the addition *global vigilance*)—continue to echo throughout Air Force strategic documents is a sign of a successful branding effort. Finally, in the process, since at least *Global Engagement,* these strategic documents accomplished yet a fourth task—encouraging a productive dialogue

---

[225] Mike Pietrucha, "America's Victory Disease Has Left It Dangerously Deluded," *War on the Rocks*, November 18, 2015.

[226] Pietrucha, 2015.

about the service's future. While different CSAFs and service secretaries have been more or less interested in publishing documents themselves over the years, that these documents have become ways for the service's senior leadership to discuss the future of the service is, perhaps, a good unto itself.

5. Lessons for Air Force Strategic Planning

The "Airpower Resources" section of the website of the Air Force Association's Mitchell Institute for Aerospace Studies has links to key strategic documents. Most of the documents there are the most recent versions of the latest national strategy documents: the 2015 *National Security Strategy*, the 2015 *National Military Strategy*, and the 2014 QDR. The Mitchell Institute also includes the four Air Force strategic documents completed under Welsh's tenure as chief— *The World's Greatest Air Force*, *America's Air Force: A Call to the Future*, the *Air Force Future Operating Concept*, and the *Strategic Master Plan*. Only two historical documents make the cut in this roster of classic Air Force strategies: *Global Reach–Global Power* (1990) and the War Department's FM 100-20 *Command and Employment of Air Power* (1943), the first doctrinal document that fully acknowledged the equal role of airpower in modern combat. This anecdote provides a telling, if unscientific, reflection of which Air Force strategic documents have stood the test of time: Arguably, only a handful of truly seminal works made a lasting effect on the service.[1]

In fairness, not all the strategies aimed to be *Global Reach—Global Power*. Indeed, there are powerful arguments in favor of stability as strategy. If the service continuously felt the need to reinvent itself with every new chief and service secretary, it would cause massive disruption to the organization's processes—especially in such areas as acquisition, which can require decades-long planning horizons. Consequently, more often than not, successive leaders build on the strategies of their predecessors to achieve narrower goals—from influencing Capitol Hill to simply encouraging an open discussion by the Air Force senior leadership about the direction of the service (see Table 5.1). Yet, as detailed above and summarized in the appendix to this report, some Air Force strategic documents proved more successful than others. The reasons for differences in effect vary by case, but, for the most part, they point to five key lessons.

---

[1] Mitchell Institute for Aerospace Studies, "Airpower Resources," undated. Data from February 25, 2016. In fairness, one could argue that such scientific studies as *Toward New Horizons* or *Project Forecast* also had long-term effects on the service by charting where Air Force research and development efforts would go and, by extension, how air warfare would be waged in the future.

Table 5.1. Air Force Strategic Documents' (1990–Present) Specified and Implied Goals

Strategy	Define Mission/Purpose	Influence Budgets	Structure the Force
Global Reach—Global Power/Blueprints for the Objective Air Force (1990)	X	X	X
Global Presence (1995)	X	X	
Global Engagement: A Vision for the 21st-Century Air Force (1996)	X		
The 1997 Air Force Long-Range Plan: Summary (1997)		X	X
America's Air Force Vision 2020: Global Vigilance, Reach, and Power (2000)	X		X
"Rapid Aerospace Dominance" (2001)	X		
The U.S. Air Force Transformation Flight Plan (2002, 2003, and 2004)		X	X
Lasting Heritage . . . Limitless Horizon: A Warfighter's Vision (2006)	X	X	X
Air Force Roadmap 2006–2025 (2006 and 2008)		X	X
The Nation's Guardians: America's 21st-Century Air Force (2007)	X	X	
2008 Air Force Strategic Plan (2008)	X	X	
CSAF Vector 2010 and *CSAF Vector 2011* (2010, 2011)	X	X	
The World's Greatest Air Force—Powered by Airmen, Fueled by Innovation: A Vision for the United States (2013)	X		
Global Vigilance, Global Reach, Global Power (2013)		X	
America's Air Force: A Call to the Future (2014)	X	X	
Air Force Future Operating Concept: A View of the Air Force in 2035 (2015)			X
Strategic Master Plan (2015)			X

Encourage Ideas from Below

The Air Force has, since its inception, enjoyed a vibrant intellectual culture, but arguably its most important works were not produced in the bowels of its bureaucracies written by committees.[2] To the contrary, historically, the Air Force's strength was its visionaries who went outside the formal confines and challenged the status quo. These free thinkers—such as Mitchell,

---

[2] Similarly, in their study of Air Force innovation, Adam R. Grissom, Caitlin Lee, and Karl P. Mueller found that unlike the other services (and specifically the Army), Air Force innovation tended to be a "more decentralized and diffuse phenomenon," originating from all over the force rather than a product of a few senior leaders at Training and Doctrine Command (Adam Grissom, Caitlin Lee, and Karl P. Mueller, *Innovation in the United States Air Force: Evidence from Six Cases*, Santa Monica, Calif.: RAND Corporation, RR-1207-AF, 2016, p. 88).

Suter, Boyd, and Warden—produced some of the Air Force's most innovative strategic works that still shape the service today.

Cultivating free thinkers who challenge accepted notions is not an easy task for any rigidly hierarchical organization such as the Air Force. As a large organization designed to operate under confusing, dangerous, and risky circumstances, the military needs discipline, rewards conservatism, and admires orthodoxy, but these are precisely the opposite traits needed to encourage innovation. In fact, whether military services are even capable of developing mavericks is the subject of much academic debate.[3] As one senior Air Force officer remarked, "really brilliant thinkers want to push the organization hard . . . [and] more often than not the bureaucracy pushes them down."[4] Another senior Air Force general officer worried, "Has it matured to the point it's becoming dogmatic as we accuse the Marine Corps? Have we matured to the point where we're no longer the creative, innovative force?"[5]

To the extent that it is possible, Air Force senior leaders need to be conscientious and protective of out-of-the-box thinkers, giving them room to write, think, and experiment. As one senior Air Force general officer remarked, "we need to encourage mavericks, risk takers, and mistake making."[6] In a performance-oriented, high-stakes organization, this is not always easy to do. Even more difficult, these senior leaders need to hear and try free thinkers' ideas for themselves. The history of Air Force strategy provides a handful of examples of this being put to practice. For example, during the early 1980s, Secretary of the Air Force Verne Orr and CSAF Gen Lew Allen encouraged senior staff to bounce out-of-the-box ideas off of them, before they were fully vetted by the entire staff process.[7] Later, Warden found an intellectual home on the Air Staff. Similarly, Rice enabled McPeak's reforms of the Air Force, and Fogleman encouraged innovation on the Long-Range Planning Board—although both of these initiatives were part of formal, rather than external, reform efforts and arguably less threatening as a result. Historical examples here are few and far between, perhaps a testament to just how difficult cultivating visionaries actually proves to be in practice.

Know Your Environment

In addition to thinking through the ideas forming their underlying message, the strategic documents also need to consider their audience. Although the lesson seems self-evident, it proves more difficult in practice. Ideally, each document can be tailored to specific objectives

---

[3] For the classic debate, see Barry P. Posen, *The Source of Military Doctrine: France, Britain and Germany Between the World Wars*, Ithaca, N.Y.: Cornell University Press, 1984; and Stephen Peter Rosen, "New Ways of War: Understanding Military Innovation," *International Security*, Vol. 13, No. 1, Summer 1998, pp. 134–168.

[4] Interview with a retired Air Force general officer, April 20, 2016.

[5] Interview with a retired senior Air Force general officer, May 11, 2016.

[6] Interview with a retired senior Air Force general officer, May 11, 2016.

[7] Interview with a retired Air Force general officer, April 20, 2016.

with a select audience. In practice, however, these documents are multivocal: They speak to multiple audiences simultaneously, often serving different purposes. Many—such as *The World's Greatest Air Force*—are largely the Air Force senior leadership talking to rank and file. Others—such as *Global Presence*—aimed to influence policy debates in Washington, D.C., and stake out new Air Force turf. Still others—such as *America's Air Force: A Call to the Future*—are signals to industry and Congress about Air Force procurement priorities.[8] They also can serve as a signal to foreign audiences about Air Force intentions.[9] Ensuring that the same document can serve all of its intended audiences simultaneously requires nuance, finesse, and, above all, knowledge of the broader policy environment.

For a document to be well-received, particularly outside of the service, it needs to fit with the context of the time in which it is produced. The 2003 *Transformation Flight Plan* suffered because its calls for space-based hypervelocity rods and airborne lasers seemed misaligned and out of touch with the strategic realities of the present time. A similar argument can be made about *The Nation's Guardians'* (2007) call to focus on high-end conventional war at the height of the Iraq War. On the merits, neither the 2003 *Transformation Flight Plan* nor *The Nation's Guardians* (2007) were wrong, per se. Especially given that many major Air Force weapon systems are developed over decades, a technology may seem irrelevant today but prove crucial tomorrow once it is actually fielded. Still, leaders need to be attuned to the seeming mismatch of resources and priorities in the here and now if they want to ensure a warm reception of their written initiatives. In contrast, *Global Presence* provides an example of possible positive effects when a service correctly judges the policy environment. Knowing that DoD and the national security community more broadly were looking for cheaper ways to maintain relationships the world over, *Global Presence* successfully sold the Air Force as being able to fulfill a role traditionally performed by the Navy, but for fewer resources. The broader policy audience took notice, and the Air Force scored a modest but consequential win.

Ultimately, understanding the environment allows strategists to identify *policy windows*—times when leaders can push their agenda through.[10] The size of the policy window varies by circumstance. Everything from external crises to the size of electoral mandates can shape how

---

[8] Interestingly, while many of the authors of these strategic documents thought they were talking to the defense industrial base, one former senior executive in a major defense contractor suggested that, for the most part, industry already knows Air Force research and development and acquisition priorities by the time these strategies are published (interviews with a retired senior Air Force general officer, January 6, 2016, and a former senior executive in a major defense contractor, April 21, 2016).

[9] Interview with a retired senior Air Force general officer, January 6, 2016.

[10] The term *policy window* comes from the political science literature. It argues that certain external factors make organizations more or less receptive to new ideas and new directions. See for example, Carol S. Weissert, "Policy Entrepreneurs, Policy Opportunists and Legislative Effectiveness," *American Political Quarterly*, Vol. 19, No. 2, April 1991; Jeff Checkel, "Ideas, Institutions, and the Gorbachev Foreign Policy Revolution," *World Politics*, Vol. 45, No. 2, January 1993; and John T. S. Keeler, "Opening the Window for Reform: Mandates, Crises, and the Extraordinary Policy-Making," *Comparative Political Studies*, Vol. 25, No. 4, January 1993.

large the policy window is and, consequently, how extensive the reforms can be.[11] While the skill and experience of the policymaker who is selling the idea matters, the circumstances also dictate how difficult this task may be. This model has been used to explain everything from state legislators' abilities to pass local law in North Carolina to Mikhail Gorbachev's ability to reform the Soviet Union.[12]

The Air Force is not a legislative body, and the CSAF is not—at least in the traditional sense of the term—a politician.[13] Yet, the same dynamics apply. Under certain circumstances, particularly when there is a significant external shock, policy windows open and allow leaders to push forward major reforms. It should come as no surprise then that the Mitchell Institute features the War Department's FM 100-20 *Command and Employment of Air Power* and *Global Reach—Global Power* (1990). The former document was drafted right as the Army Air Corps was about to demonstrate the effects of strategic bombing; the latter came at the end of the Cold War, when the Air Force was restructuring itself for a unipolar age. The historical opportunities do not come around often, but when they do, the Air Force strategic documents can have outsized effect at focusing the future of the force. Conversely, when the service is not at these critical junctures, these documents may be less relevant. Understanding when a "policy window" opens, however, requires strategists to be aware of the dynamics shaping the policy environment beyond their offices and, indeed, beyond the service itself.

Develop Strategy from the Top

Although ideas can come from anywhere and the knowledge of policy environment can be informed by public and congressional relations staff, strategy—the actual plan for where the service is headed—needs to start at the top.[14] Strategy cannot be delegated out to a division on the Air Staff or outside consulting firms. Indeed, as the death of "Rapid Aerospace Dominance" demonstrates—if the senior-most levels of leadership do not buy the plan, the strategy dies. In fact, in many cases, senior leadership is often integrally involved in the development of a plan from the start. One former CSAF remarked about his tenure, "Everyone kept telling me I had to have a long-range planning staff. I told those people '[expletive] you. I'm doing it myself.'"[15] Another former Secretary of the Air Force expressed similar sentiments, although with less profane language. During his time, he needed to "own" strategic planning, since only he—and

---

[11] Keeler, 1993, p. 437.

[12] Weissert, 1991; Chekel, 1993.

[13] Arguably, this may prescribe a larger role for the Secretary of the Air Force in crafting these public documents, since as a political appointee, ideally, he or she should be attuned to what "policy windows" are open at the time.

[14] Other studies note the importance of strategy in driving Air Force innovation, particularly for connecting the strategic with operational problems and then resourcing the effort accordingly. See Grissom, Lee, and Mueller, 2016, p. 86.

[15] Interview with a retired senior Air Force general officer, April 14, 2016.

the senior Air Force uniformed leadership—had the experience and institutional power to plan and execute long-term strategy. He felt that the staff simply should flesh out what the senior leader already decided.[16]

An interesting question here is: Who at the top should drive strategy? Previous studies often focus on the central role of the CSAF in long-range planning, usually citing Fogleman's part in the creation of *Global Engagement* and the *Long-Range Plan*.[17] While true, Air Force history is also studded with examples of powerful service secretaries—such as Eugene Zuckert, John Stetson, or Donald Rice—driving the process. These civilian leaders rose above the din and pushed the service to confront strategic issues it either could not or did not want to see and articulated a vision that the service could not. By contrast, most of the more recent service secretaries and chiefs interviewed for this project suggested that they shared the role of strategist-in-chief among them. Ultimately, history does not necessarily provide a clear guide for what arrangement works best: Theoretically, the chief's deep institutional knowledge should complement the service secretaries' outsider perspectives, but, in practice, this is not always the case.

No matter who at the top drives the strategy-making progress, eventually everyone at the top needs to be on the same page. As a result, the lynchpin for Air Force strategy documents' success often is getting senior leaders to buy into a plan for two reasons. First, to change an organization as large and decentralized as the Air Force, the plan needs to be socialized with the Air Force senior leadership to turn the plan into reality. Perhaps the best example of this need comes from Fogleman's approach to *Global Engagement*. By successfully socializing the proposals with his fellow four stars, Fogleman managed to introduce some controversial reforms, including the Air Force's further embrace of UAVs. Second and perhaps more importantly, the process of getting key leader buy-in may be a good in and of itself. Even if the strategic document produces only marginal changes, there arguably is a benefit to forcing all the Air Force senior leadership to engage in a discussion about where the service is headed.

Although the potential benefits of key leader buy-in are fairly clear, how to gain this universal commitment in practice proves more difficult. Fogleman's experience with *Global Engagement* provides a partial answer. First, Fogleman demonstrated his own personal commitment to the effort by assigning senior staff to develop the work and insisting the Air Forces' major commands do the same. Second, Fogleman included the other Air Force four stars in the development of the strategy via the 1996 Corona conference, which ensured that they were equally vested in the outcome. Fogleman then briefed the concept all over the Air Force. Ultimately, the best test of the degree of key leader buy-in comes only after the CSAF's turnover: When Fogleman's successor, Michael Ryan, stated that he too believed that *Global*

---

[16] Interview with a senior Air Force leader, April 21, 2016.

[17] For example, Barzelay and Campbell, 2003.

Engagement was "fundamentally sound" and argued that "it's now up to us to go out and execute it," he demonstrated that the Air Force as whole had accepted *Global Engagement*.[18]

Importantly, while *Global Engagement* provides a model, it does not provide an ironclad recipe for attaining key leader buy-in. Structurally, Ryan tried to follow many of the same steps that Fogleman did in *America's Air Force Vision 2020*, including using the Corona conference to help socialize the ideas within the strategy. And yet, whether it was for reasons of timing or because Ryan did not have Fogleman's passion for strategic planning, Ryan's document generally received lower marks. Ultimately, gaining key leader buy-in may be more art than science.

Keep the Strategy Succinct, Substantive, and Sharp

Unclassified Air Force strategy documents often need to navigate two extremes—between being too much of a public relations pamphlet and too dry and esoteric. Starting at least with the 1979 version of the *Basic Doctrine* but particularly since the beginning of the 21st century, the Air Force arguably opted increasingly for style over substance—filling these strategic documents with motivational but tangential photographs, quotes from historical Air Force leaders, and strategic platitudes. Although this may make these documents more visibly attention-grabbing and better public-relations pamphlets, this added flash arguably muddles the documents' message and its plan for the way ahead for the service. By contrast, other strategic documents suffered almost from the other extreme. As one senior strategic planner noted, some documents are so detailed that they "sit on the shelf and collect dust" and the "metrics [used to measure progress] were so convoluted that nobody could make sense of them."[19] Once the strategic documents balloon to dozens of pages containing hundreds of tasks and subtasks, they lose their clarity and effect.[20]

Successful—or at least influential—strategy documents require a clear if blunt vision for the service defended by details and measured by a handful of select documents about how the Air Force will fulfill its priorities, with few additional distractors. Indeed, many of the most influential strategic documents—be it Arnold's *Air Power and the Future* or *Global Reach—Global Power*—were stylistically relatively simple documents. More recently, *America's Air Force: A Call to the Future* is stylistically a simpler document than its two immediate predecessors, *The World's Greatest Air Force* and *Global Vigilance, Global Reach, Global Power*. And yet, *America's Air Force* gives a fairly clear picture of where the Air Force wants to go—and conversely not go—in terms of force structure and procurement priorities and

---

[18] Tirpak, 1998, p. 38.

[19] Interview with a retired Air Force general officer, April 27, 2016.

[20] Interview with a retired senior Air Force general officer, January 6, 2016; and interview with a retired Air Force general officer, April 27, 2016.

consequently was better received and was more effective than either of its predecessors. A similar lesson can be drawn from *The Nation's Guardians*, which attracted attention not for its elaborate layout but for its clear focus on conventional threats and its justification for the need for high-end capabilities—such as the F-22 Raptor—to combat them. If Moseley intended to raise concern about the Air Force falling behind its near-peer competitors, the document proved successful.

Ultimately, as this report has argued, institutional strategies usually have three aims: advocating and providing top-level guidance for future budget priorities, shaping the force, and defining the identity of the service. Writing good strategies also starts with recognizing the objective or objectives the strategy hopes to accomplish and then succinctly, substantively, and sharply writing to those objectives, all the while minimizing the numbers of distractors and extraneous information in the process.

Focus on the Process as Much as the Product

Finally, Air Force strategists need to recognize that often the value of strategic documents comes as much from the process behind these documents' creation as from the documents itself. Despite the hours of staff work that went into these documents originally, when asked about what they viewed as important in the documents some ten or 15 years later, many senior leaders downplayed much of what is in the documents written under their tenures. Reflecting on *America's Air Force Vision 2020*, one senior leader remarked that much of the value was the single page of the document explaining the Aerospace Expeditionary Force.[21] Another senior leader suggested that most of *Global Engagement*'s true value was the handful of lines on shifting from "air and space" to a "space and air force" and then identifying core values.[22] Others suggested that the most important part of *Global Reach—Global Power* was its title.

Instead, most of the senior leaders interviewed for this report viewed the process as the jewel of strategic planning. Most particularly valued the opportunity for the Air Force senior leadership—from across the disparate parts of the Air Force representing each of its different major commands—to come together and develop, if not a common approach, then at least a common set of messages that could be sold throughout the service. The process, however, should extend beyond the four-star ranks and the Corona gatherings. As Fogleman's experience with *Global Engagement* demonstrates, these documents offer an opportunity to solicit views from across the force and help build a consensus around the direction of the service and to the collective identity of the service itself. Viewed in this light, most of the value of strategic planning may come before one of these documents ever goes to press. So rather than getting caught up in the minutia of these documents, Air Force strategists perhaps should be more

---

[21] Interview with an Air Force senior leader, May 9, 2016.

[22] Interview with an Air Force senior leader, May 5, 2016.

concerned about the discussions these documents spark, rather than necessarily what these documents say.

6. Postscript: The Future of Air Force Strategy

Going forward, the Air Force will face new limitations when it comes to producing strategies. Under congressional pressure, the Air Force, like its sister services, will need to cut 25 percent of its headquarters staff.[1] As a result, the Air Force will need to be more strategic about how it uses its limited staffing resources and determine which of these public strategies are actually worth producing. During his tenure as Secretary of Defense, Robert Gates tried to push the entire DoD in that direction and maintained that each report include its full-burdened cost on its cover as a way of prompting the bureaucracy to think about how much each of these reports are actually worth.[2] Gates's effort failed and was ultimately abandoned. That said, there is a question that if resources—in terms of finances and manhours—become scarcer, would DoD as a whole, and the Air Force in particular, need to reconsider the policy?

Even if not pushed, the Air Force should consider reforming the way it does long-term strategy. While many of the former strategic planners interviewed for this project touted the importance of long-term planning and planning processes, many of the service secretaries and CSAFs expressed more skepticism of the endeavor. Indeed, many of these senior leaders doubted their ability to predict and plan decades out in a concrete sense.

This does not necessarily mean that the Air Force should abandon long-term planning altogether, but the service secretaries, CSAFs, and other senior leaders' general skepticism about these strategic documents' utility should warn the service to be more circumspect. Written by committee, formal strategic documents rarely will be as innovative or as creative as documents produced by mavericks free of these bureaucratic constraints. Similarly, formal documents rarely can produce wholesale change. The Air Force is simply too large an institution, beholden to too many different constituencies inside and outside the service, to change quickly. And as with anything that claims to predict the future, strategic documents are often premised on a fair deal of uncertainty.

Yet, Air Force strategic planning has shown that it can accomplish certain, more modest ends. First, strategies can help justify resources. Indeed, the Air Force historically has proven fairly adept at undertaking large-scale scientific reviews—such as *Toward New Horizons* or *Project Forecast*—and then using their results about what technologies are within the realm of possibility to guide research, development, and procurement. Second, strategic plans can help structure the force. Occasionally, the circumstances allow for wholesale changes to Air Force structure, as occurred with the *Blueprints for the Objective Force.* More often, strategies allow for more-modest changes—such as with Aerospace Expeditionary Forces in *America's Air Force*

---

[1] Clark, 2015.

[2] Interview with a retired senior Air Force general officer, January 6, 2016.

Vision 2020. Third, strategic documents help explain the institution's roles, mission, and, arguably, even its culture. From its initial attempts to write the need for an independent air branch during World War II in AWPD-1 and FM 100-20 to more-recent attempts to secure the Air Force's uniqueness in *Global Presence* and *Global Vigilance, Global Reach, Global Power for America* (2013), strategic documents have sought to define and defend the Air Force's bureaucratic turf.

Perhaps most importantly, strategic planning creates a helpful dialogue within the service and particularly among its senior leaders about the direction of the service—even if it only yields lackluster results in the end. This is why the lessons outlined in the previous chapter are critical. Understanding these five basic lessons may not allow the Air Force to produce better strategy, but it may allow it to make the most out of the process. And, every so often, when the right confluence of ideas, leadership, and policy windows align, the Air Force strategic plans may, indeed, produce real change.

Appendix. Effect of Specific Air Force Strategic Documents

This table details the Air Force strategic documents produced after the Cold War and their relative effect as defined in Chapter Five.

Table A.1. Effect of U.S. Air Force Strategic Documents (1990–Present)

Strategy	Results
Global Reach—Global Power/Blueprints for the Objective Air Force (1990)	• *Readership:* Widespread readership throughout the Air Force (there were even plans for a bumper sticker) • *Resource shifts:* Major organizational changes to the Air Force; senior officer rank restructure • *Permanence:* Many of the resource shifts remain in place today
Global Presence (1995)	• *Readership:* Limited policy audience • *Resource shifts:* Carved out policy space to the Air Force to assume the presence mission, but less effect on force structure or resource allocation • *Permanence:* Not observable
Global Engagement: A Vision for the 21st-Century Air Force (1996)	• *Readership:* Widespread readership within the Air Force, especially among the senior leadership • *Resource shifts:* Modest effect on resources (particularly UAVs and space) • *Permanence:* Air Force values and core competencies continue; focus on space and UAVs continued after Fogleman's tenure
The 1997 Air Force Long-Range Plan: Summary (1997)	• *Readership:* Less attention outside of Air Force channels • *Resource shifts:* Struggled to identify offsets to pay for modernization • *Permanence:* Focus on space and UAVs continued after Fogleman's tenure
America's Air Force Vision 2020: Global Vigilance, Reach, and Power (2000)	• *Readership:* Less attention than either *Global Reach—Global Power* or *Global Engagement* • *Resources:* Committed the Air Force to the Aerospace Expeditionary Force • *Permanence:* The Aerospace Expeditionary Force exists in some form today
"Rapid Aerospace Dominance"	• *Readership:* N/A (never published) • *Resources:* N/A (never implemented) • *Permanence:* None
The U.S. Air Force Transformation Flight Plan (2002, 2003, and 2004)	• *Readership:* Negative attention in the popular press; minimal attention in the scholarly press • *Resources:* Some of the more futuristic programs were later canceled • *Permanence:* None

Strategy	Results
Lasting Heritage . . . Limitless Horizon: A Warfighter's Vision (2006)	• *Readership:* Internal Air Force audience • *Resource shifts:* Mandated shifts in resources, which ultimately occurred • *Permanence:* General shifts in resources occurred, but the vision itself has largely been forgotten
Air Force Roadmap 2006–2025 (2006 and, 2008)	• *Readership:* Generated positive coverage in the local press (helping protect Air Force procurement programs) • *Resources:* Minimal effect on transforming the Air Force as an institution • *Permanence:* Many of the procurement programs continued
The Nation's Guardians: America's 21st-Century Air Force (2007)	• *Readership:* Ample public attention, mostly because it did not align with the Secretary of Defense's priorities • *Resource shifts:* None • *Permanence:* None
2008 Air Force Strategic Plan (2008)	• *Readership:* Primarily internal audience • *Resource shifts:* None • *Permanence:* No observable effect
CSAF Vector 2010 and *CSAF Vector 2011* (2010 and 2011)	• *Readership:* Primarily internal audience, with some public coverage • *Resource shifts:* Modest redirection of resources • *Permanence:* No observable effect
The World's Greatest Air Force— Powered by Airmen, Fueled by Innovation: A Vision for the United States (2013)	• *Readership:* Primarily internal audience, with some public coverage • *Resource shifts:* None • *Permanence:* To be determined
Global Vigilance, Global Reach, Global Power (2013)	• *Readership:* Modest readership (based on YouTube views, press releases, etc.) • *Resource shifts:* None • *Permanence:* To be determined
America's Air Force: A Call to the Future (2014)	• *Readership:* Inside the Air Force, but also reached a broader policy audience • *Resource shifts:* Laid out clear funding priorities, but less clear if they were ultimately enacted • *Permanence:* To be determined
Air Force Future Operating Concept: A View of the Air Force in 2035 (2015)	• *Readership:* Internal with some external audience (to the defense policy world) • *Resource shifts:* To be determined • *Permanence:* To be determined
Strategic Master Plan (2015)	• To be determined

References

Air Force Association, *Global Reach—Global Power: The Evolving Air Force Contribution to National Security*, Arlington, Va., December 1992.

Air Force News Service, "AF Leaders Cite Airmen as Bedrock in New Core Mission Document," August 22, 2013a. As of February 24, 2016:
http://www.af.mil/News/ArticleDisplay/tabid/223/Article/466921/af-leaders-cite-airmen-as-bedrock-in-new-core-mission-document.aspx

———, "Every Airman Matters, Each Story Is Important," August 29, 2013b. As of February 24, 2016:
http://www.hilltoptimes.com/content/every-airman-matters-each-story-important

Air Force Office of Scientific Research, "A Brief Organizational History," Wright-Patterson Air Force Base website, July 17, 2016. As of October 27, 2016:
http://www.wpafb.af.mil/Welcome/Fact-Sheets/Display/Article/842007

Air Force Personnel Center, "Air Force Personnel Demographics," September 30, 2016. As of October 27, 2016:
http://www.afpc.af.mil/Air-Force-Demographics

Air Force Public Affairs Agency, "Strategic Agility Is the Future of the Air Force," July 30, 2014. As of February 25, 2016:
http://www.af.mil/News/ArticleDisplay/tabid/223/Article/486897/strategic-agility-is-the-future-of-the-air-force.aspx

Allen, Jerrod P., "Institutionalizing Long Range Planning," in Perry M. Smith, Jerrold P. Allen, John H. Stewart II, and F. Douglas Whitehouse, eds., *Creating Strategic Vision: Long-Range Planning for National Security*, Washington, D.C.: National Defense University Press, 1987. As of April 20, 2016:
http://www.dtic.mil/dtic/tr/fulltext/u2/a187043.pdf

Arnold, Henry H., "Air Power and the Future," in Eugene M. Emme, ed., *The Impact of Air Power: National Security and World Politics*, Princeton, N.J.: D. Van Nostrand Company, Inc., 1959.

Aspin, Les, *Report of the Bottom-Up Review*, Washington, D.C.: U.S. Department of Defense, October 1993. As of July 5, 2016:
http://www.dtic.mil/cgi-bin/GetTRDoc?AD=ADA359953

Axe, David, "Air Force's Big 'Roadmap' Tease," *Wired*, January 17, 2008a. As of January 22, 2016:
http://www.wired.com/2008/01/air-forces-big/

———, "Army Strategy Manual Gets It Right," *Wired*, February 27, 2008b. As of January 13, 2016:
http://www.wired.com/2008/02/army-strategy-m/

Barry, John, "Rapid Aerospace Dominance: A Unifying Concept for the Air Force," unpublished briefing, July 2001.

Barzelay, Michael, and Colin Campbell, *Preparing for the Future: Strategic Planning in the U.S. Air Force*, Washington, D.C.: Brooking Institution Press, July 31, 2003.

Berger, Alexander, "Beyond Blue Four: The Past and Future Transformation of Red Flag," *Air and Space Power Journal*, Vol. 19, No. 2, Summer 2005, pp. 43–54.

Bookman, Jay, "U.S. Planning for the War It Wishes For," *Atlanta Journal-Constitution*, May 19, 2005, p. 19A.

Bowman, Tom, "Air Force Chief Resigns over Disputes '97 Terrorist Bombing Was Source of Division," *Baltimore Sun*, July 29, 1997. As of July 11, 2016:
http://articles.baltimoresun.com/1997-07-29/news/1997210031_1_air-force-fogleman-force-chief

Broder, John M., "Air Force Chief Fired by Cheney," *Los Angeles Times*, September 18, 1990. As of July 15, 2016:
http://articles.latimes.com/1990-09-18/news/mn-585_1_air-force-official

Bronfeld, Saul, "Fighting Outnumbered: The Impact of the Yom Kippur War on the U.S. Army," *Journal of Military History*, Vol. 71, No. 2, April 2007, pp. 465–498.

Brown, Michael E., "The U.S. Manned Bomber and Strategic Deterrence in the 1990s," *International Security*, Vol. 14, No. 2, Fall 1989, pp. 4–45.

Butler, George L., "Adjusting to Post–Cold War Strategic Realities," *Parameters*, Spring 1991, pp. 2–9.

Byman, Daniel L., and Matthew C. Waxman, "Kosovo and the Great Air Power Debate," *International Security*, Vol. 24, No. 4, Spring 2000, pp. 5–38.

Campbell, Colin, "Long-Range Corporate Strategic Planning in Government Organizations: The Case of the U.S. Air Force," *Governance*, Vol. 15, No. 4, October 2002, pp. 425–453.

"Cannon Addresses 'Air Force Roadmap,'" *Clovis News Journal*, January 16, 2008. As of April 11, 2016:
http://www.cnjonline.com/2008/01/16/cannon-addresses-air-force-roadmap/

Checkel, Jeff, "Ideas, Institutions, and the Gorbachev Foreign Policy Revolution," *World Politics*, Vol. 45, No. 2, January 1993, pp. 271–300.

Cheng, Joey, "Air Force's 30-Year Plan Seeks 'Strategic Agility,'" *Defense Systems*, July 31, 2014. As of February 25, 2016:
https://defensesystems.com/articles/2014/07/31/air-force-30-year-strategy.aspx

Chu, Carolyn, Brandon Dues, and Laura L. Miller, *Cultural Themes in Messages from Top Air Force Leaders, 2005–2008*, Santa Monica, Calif.: RAND Corporation, DB-583-AF, 2010. As of January 25, 2016:
http://www.rand.org/pubs/documented_briefings/DB583.html

Clark, Charles, "Pentagon Orders Even More HQ Cuts, Infuriating Employees' Union," *Defense One*, September 9, 2015. As of February 26, 2016:
http://www.defenseone.com/management/2015/09/pentagon-orders-even-more-hq-cuts-infuriating-employees-union/120548/

Cohen, Raphael S., "A Tale of Two Manuals," *Prism*, Vol. 2, No. 1, December 2011, pp. 87–100.

Coram, Robert, *Boyd: The Fighter Pilot Who Changed the Art of War*, Boston: Little, Brown and Company, 2002.

Council on Foreign Relations, "Air Force Weapon System Roadmap," January 16, 2008. As of April 11, 2016:
http://www.cfr.org/world/air-force-weapon-system-roadmap/p15307

David, Leonard, "Air Force Plans for Future War in Space," NBC News, February 23, 2004. As March 14, 2016:
http://www.nbcnews.com/id/4353309/ns/technology_and_science-space/t/air-force-plans-future-war-space/

DoD—*See* U.S. Department of Defense.

Douhet, Giulio, *Command of the Air*, trans. Dino Ferrari, Washington, D.C.: Air Force History and Museums Program, 1998. As of February 11, 2016:
http://www.au.af.mil/au/awc/awcgate/readings/command_of_the_air.pdf

Dowdy, William L., *Testing the Aerospace Expeditionary Force Concept: An Analysis of AEFs I–IV (1995–97) and the Way Ahead*, Maxwell Air Force Base, Ala.: College of Aerospace Doctrine, Research and Education, Air University, Research Paper 2000-01, 2000. As of January 27, 2016:
http://www.dtic.mil/cgi-bin/GetTRDoc?AD=ADA381886

Drape, James H., "Building Partnership Capacity: Operation Harmattan and Beyond," *Air and Space Power Journal*, September–October 2012, pp. 65–93.

Dryden, H. L., G. A. Morton, I. A. Getting, *Guidance and Homing of Missiles and Pilotless Aircraft: A Report for the AAF Scientific Advisory Group*, Vol. 9, Dayton, Ohio: Wright Field, May 1946. As of November 3, 2016:
http://www.governmentattic.org/vonK/
GuideHomingMissilesPilotlessAcft_VKarman_V9.pdf

Dryden, H. L., W. H. Pickering, H. S. Tsien, and G. B. Schubauer, *Guided Missiles and Pilotless Aircraft: A Report Prepared for the AAF Scientific Advisory Group*, Vol. 8, Dayton, Ohio: Wright Field, May 1946. As of November 3, 2016:
http://www.governmentattic.org/vonK/MissilesPilotlessAcft_VKarman_VB.pdf

Dubridge, L. A., E. M. Purcell, G. A. Morton, and G. E. Valley, *Radar and Communications: A Report Prepared for the AAF Scientific Advisory Group*, Vol. 11, Dayton, Ohio: Wright Field, May 1946. As of November 3, 2016:
http://www.governmentattic.org/vonK/RadarAndCommunications_VKarman_V11.pdf

Eaglen, Mackenzie, "Air Force Delivers New and Innovative Vision of Future Warfare," *Real Clear Defense*, September 15, 2015. As of February 26, 2016:
http://www.realcleardefense.com/articles/2015/09/15/
air_force_delivers_new_and_innovative_vision_of_future_warfare_108468.html

Ehrhard, Thomas P., *An Air Force Strategy for the Long Haul*, Washington, D.C.: Center for Strategic and Budgetary Assessments, 2009.

———, *Air Force UAVs: The Secret History*, Arlington, Va.: The Mitchell Institute, 2010. As of January 27, 2016:
http://www.dtic.mil/cgi-bin/GetTRDoc?AD=ADA525674

Faulkenberry, Barbara J., *Global Reach—Global Power: Air Force Strategic Vision, Past and Future*, Maxwell Air Force Base, Ala.: Air University Press, 1996.

Fogleman, Ronald R., "Statement for General Ronald R. Fogleman Chief of Staff, U.S. Air Force," 1997. As of January 12, 2016:
http://fas.org/man/congress/1997/h970522f.htm

Fogleman, Ronald. R., and Sheila E. Widnall, *Global Engagement: A Vision for the 21st-Century Air Force*, 1996. As of January 14, 2016:
http://www.au.af.mil/au/awc/awcgate/global/global.pdf

Fontaine, Scott, "Schwartz: Way Ahead Includes Modernization, International Cooperation," *Air Force Times*, July 27, 2010, p. 21. As of November 10, 2016:
http://search.proquest.com/military/docview/740985027/920ABE9163164531PQ/25?account id=25333

Freedberg, Sydney J., Jr., "Air Force to Focus on High-Threat Future, If Congress Lets It: James and Welsh," *Breaking Defense*, July 30, 2014. As of February 25, 2016: http://breakingdefense.com/2014/07/air-force-must-focus-on-high-threat-future-if-congress-will-let-it-james-welsh/

Futrell, Robert Frank, *Ideas, Concepts, Doctrine: Basic Thinking in the United States Air Force, 1907–1960*, Vol. 1, Maxwell Air Force Base, Ala.: Air University Press, December 1989a.

———, *Ideas, Concepts, Doctrine: Basic Thinking in the United States Air Force, 1907–1960*, Vol. 2, Maxwell Air Force Base, Ala.: Air University Press, 1989b.

Gates, Robert, *Duty: Memoirs of a Secretary at War*, New York: Alfred A. Knopf, 2014.

Gordon, Michael R., "Report by Powell Challenges Calls to Revise Military," *New York Times*, December 31, 1992. As of January 14, 2016: http://www.nytimes.com/1992/12/31/us/report-by-powell-challenges-calls-to-revise-military.html

Gorn, Michael H., ed., *Prophecy Fulfilled: "Toward New Horizons" and Its Legacy*, Washington, D.C.: Air Force History and Museums Program, 1994. As of July 5, 2016: http://www.afhso.af.mil/shared/media/document/AFD-100928-066.pdf

Grant, Rebecca, "The Redefinition of Strategic Airpower," *Air Force Magazine*, October 2003. As of May 6, 2016: http://www.airforcemag.com/MagazineArchive/Pages/2003/October%202003/1003strategic.aspx

———, "End of the Cold War Air Force," *Air Force Magazine*, July 2012, pp. 40–44. As of October 27, 2016: http://www.airforcemag.com/MagazineArchive/Pages/2012/July%202012/0712coldwar.aspx

Grier, Peter, "Air Force Peers into Future; Sees 'Smart' Helmets, Radars in Space," *Christian Science Monitor*, April 24, 1986. As of April 20, 2016: http://www.csmonitor.com/1986/0424/jforce.html

Grissom, Adam R., Caitlin Lee, and Karl P. Mueller, *Innovation in the United States Air Force: Evidence from Six Cases*, Santa Monica, Calif.: RAND Corporation, RR-1207-AF, 2016. As of July 5, 2016: http://www.rand.org/pubs/research_reports/RR1207.html

Hallion, Richard P., *Storm over Iraq: Air Power and the Gulf War*, Washington, D.C.: Smithsonian Institution Press, 1992.

Hansell, Haywood S., Jr., *The Air Plan That Defeated Hitler*, Atlanta, Ga.: Higgins-McArthur/Longino and Porter, Inc., 1972.

———, *The Strategic Air Plan Against Germany and Japan: A Memoir*, Washington, D.C.: Office of Air Force History, United States Air Force, 1986.

Hays, Peter, and Karl Mueller, "Going Boldly—Where? Aerospace Integration, the Space Commission, and the Air Force's Vision for Space," *Aerospace Power Journal*, Spring 2001, pp. 34–49. As of February 11, 2016:
http://www.airpower.maxwell.af.mil/airchronicles/apj/apj01/spr01/mueller.pdf

Headquarters, U.S. Air Force/Future Concepts and Transformation Division, *The U.S. Air Force Transformation Flight Plan*, November 2003. As of January 22, 2016:
http://www.au.af.mil/au/awc/awcgate/af/af_trans_flightplan_nov03.pdf

———, *The U.S. Air Force Transformation Flight Plan*, 2004. As of September 13, 2016:
http://www.iwar.org.uk/rma/resources/usaf/transformation-flight-plan-2004.pdf

Holmes, Sue Major, "Three N.M. Bases Getting New Planes Under USAF 'Road Map,'" Associated Press, January 16, 2008. As of January 22, 2016:
http://www.abqjournal.com/news/apafmap01-16-08.htm

Huck, Peter, "The Race of the Space Warriors," *New Zealand Herald*, September 22, 2006. As of October 27, 2016:
http://www.nzherald.co.nz/world/news/article.cfm?c_id=2&objectid=10402555

Jackovics, Ted, "MacDill in the Running for New Flying Tankers," *Tampa Tribune*, February 15, 2008. As of January 22, 2016:
http://www.tbo.com/news/metro/2008/feb/15/me-aircraft-fuel-military-hopes-planes-part-of-mod-ar-153019/

Kagan, Fredrick W., *Finding the Target: The Transformation of the American Military Policy*, New York: Encounter Books, 2006.

Keeler, John T. S., "Opening the Window for Reform: Mandates, Crises, and the Extraordinary Policy-Making," *Comparative Political Studies*, Vol. 25, No. 4, January 1993, pp. 433–486.

Krepon, Michael, "A Case Study in Policy Entrepreneurship," Washington, D.C.: The Stimson Center, undated. As of October 27, 2016:
https://www.yumpu.com/en/document/view/26749070/a-case-study-in-policy-entrepreneurship-the-stimson-center

Krick, Irving P., *War and Weather: A Report Prepared for the AAF Scientific Advisory Group*, Dayton, Ohio: Wright Field, May 1946.

Lallanilla, Marc, "Shooting Stars," ABC News, March 30, 2004. As of March 14, 2016:
http://abcnews.go.com/Health/Technology/story?id=165290&page=1

Lambeth, Benjamin S., *The Transformation of American Air Power*, Ithaca, N.Y.: Cornell University Press, 2000.

———, *Mastering the Ultimate High Ground: Next Steps in the Military Uses of Space*, Santa Monica, Calif.: RAND Corporation, MR-1649-AF, 2003. As of April 12, 2016: http://www.rand.org/pubs/monograph_reports/MR1649.html

LaPlante, William A., and Burton M. Field, "Fiscal Year 2015 Combat Aviation Programs," Washington, D.C.: Department of the Air Force Presentation to the House Armed Services Committee Subcommittee on Tactical Air and Land Forces, March 26, 2014. As of January 25, 2016: http://docs.house.gov/meetings/AS/AS25/20140326/101954/HHRG-113-AS25-Wstate-LaPlanteW-20140326.pdf

Lee, Caitlin, *The Culture of U.S. Air Force Innovation: A Historical Case Study of the Predator Program*, doctoral dissertation, London: Kings College, 2016.

Levins, Harry, "Flying High . . . 'Big Bomb' Takes a Back Seat in the New Air Force," *St. Louis Post-Dispatch*, September 22, 1991, p. 1C.

Lewis, Kevin N., *The U.S. Air Force Budget and Posture over Time*, Santa Monica, Calif.: RAND Corporation, R-3807-AF, 1990. As of October 27, 2016: http://www.rand.org/pubs/reports/R3807.html

Livingston, Thomas K., *Building the Capacity of Partner States Through Security Force Assistance*," Washington, D.C.: Congressional Research Service, R41817, May 5, 2011. As of January 25, 2016: https://www.fas.org/sgp/crs/natsec/R41817.pdf

Lovelace, W. R., A. P. Gagge, and C. W. Bray, *Aviation Medicine and Psychology: A Report Prepared for the AAF Scientific Advisory Group*, Dayton, Ohio: Wright Field, May 1946.

Lowther, Adam, "A Year Later: Responding to Problems in the ICBM Force," *Bulletin of the Atomic Scientists*, February 12, 2015. As of July 15, 2016: http://thebulletin.org/year-later-responding-problems-icbm-force7984

Mac Dougall, D. P., and N. M. Newmark, *Explosives and Terminal Ballistics: A Report Prepared for the AAF Scientific Advisory Group*, Vol. 10, Dayton, Ohio: Wright Field, May 1946. As of November 3, 2016: http://www.governmentattic.org/vonK/ExplosivesTerminalBallistics_VKarman_V10.pdf

Mayer, John D., Jr., and William P. Myers, *Meeting Future Airlift Requirements: Briefing on Preliminary Analysis of Costs of Alternative Approaches*, Washington, D.C.: Congressional Budget Office, March 1984. As of March 10, 2016: https://www.cbo.gov/sites/default/files/98th-congress-1983-1984/reports/1984_03_airlift.pdf

McGarry, Brendan, "Congress to Air Force: Push to Retire A-10 'Misguided,'" *DoD Buzz*, September 30, 2015. As of February 25, 2016:
http://www.dodbuzz.com/2015/09/30/congress-to-air-force-push-to-retire-a-10-misguided/

McPeak, Merrill A., *Selected Works of Merrill A. McPeak: 1990–1994*, Maxwell Air Force Base, Ala.: Air University Press, August 1995. As of October 27, 2016:
http://www.dtic.mil/cgi-bin/GetTRDoc?AD=ADA421979

Meilinger, Phillip S., "The Problem with Our Air Power Doctrine," *Air Power Journal*, Spring 1992. As of January 12, 2016:
http://www.airpower.maxwell.af.mil/airchronicles/apj/apj92/spr92/meiling.htm

Mitchell Institute for Aerospace Studies, "Airpower Resources," undated. As of February 25, 2016:
http://www.mitchellaerospacepower.org/#!resources/c1a4e

Moody, Walton S., and Jacob Neufeld, "Modernizing After Vietnam," in Bernard C. Nalty, ed., *Winged Sword, Winged Shield: A History of the United States Air Force 1950–1997*, Vol. II, Washington, D.C.: Air Force History and Museums Program, United States Air Force, 1997.

Moorhead, Glen W. III, *Global Reach—Global Power and the USAF Tactical Air Forces*, Carlisle Barracks, Pa.: U.S. Army War College, April 15, 1991. As of October 27, 2016:
http://www.dtic.mil/dtic/tr/fulltext/u2/a237060.pdf

Moseley, T. Michael, *The Nation's Guardians: America's 21st-Century Air Force*, Chief of Staff, U.S. Air Force white paper, December 29, 2007.

Mowbray, James A., "Air Force Doctrine Problems: 1926–Present," *Air and Space Power Journal*, Winter 1995, pp. 2–17.

Murdock, Clark A., "Forging the Vision: An Intellectual History of the Post–Cold War Air Force," draft working paper, 2001.

———, "The Search for a Systemic Solution: Air Force Planning Since the Persian Gulf War," working paper, 2002.

Myers, Gene, "Global Reach—Global Power: A Stillborn Doctrine," *Defense Analysis*, Vol. 8, No. 3, 1992, pp. 319–321.

Oberdorfer, Don, "Strategy for Solo Superpower: Pentagon Looks to 'Regional Contingencies,'" *Washington Post*, May 19, 1991, p. A1.

Parnell, Gregory S., Richard L. Eilers, Philip A. Richard, Steve P. Doucet, John A. Rolando, Larry D. Autry, Gregg M. Burgess, Patricia M. Fornes, Patrick J. Thomas, and John L. Burkhart, *Methodology for Analyzing Global Reach—Global Power*, white paper,

Washington, D.C.: Air Force Center for Studies and Analyses, the Pentagon, October 11, 1990.

Pietrucha, Mike, "America's Victory Disease Has Left It Dangerously Deluded," *War on the Rocks*, November 18, 2015. As of February 26, 2016: http://warontherocks.com/2015/11/americas-victory-disease-has-left-it-dangerously-deluded/

Posen, Barry P., *The Source of Military Doctrine: France, Britain and Germany Between the World Wars*, Ithaca, N.Y.: Cornell University Press, 1984.

President's Air Policy Commission, *Survival in the Air Age: A Report by the President's Air Policy Commission*, Washington D.C.: U.S. Government Printing Office, January 1, 1948. As of February 18, 2016: https://archive.org/details/survivalinairage00unitrich

Press, Daryl G., "The Myth of Air Power in the Persian Gulf War and the Future of Warfare," *International Security*, Vol. 26, No. 2, Fall 2001, pp. 5–44.

Reynolds, Richard T., *Heart of the Storm: The Genesis of the Air Campaign Against Iraq*, Maxwell Air Force Base, Ala.: Air University Press, January 1995. As of March 22, 2016: http://www.au.af.mil/au/awc/awcgate/au/reynolds.pdf

Rice, Donald B., *The Air Force and U.S. National Security: Global Reach—Global Power*, white paper, Washington, D.C.: Department of the Air Force, June 1990a. As of March 10, 2016: https://secure.afa.org/EdOp/2012/GRGP_Rice_1990.pdf

———, "The Manned Bomber and Strategic Deterrence: The U.S. Air Force Perspective," *International Security*, Vol. 15, No. 1, Summer 1990b, pp. 100–128.

Ricks, Thomas E., "Air Force Says It Can Offer 'Presence' in Peacetime at Lower Cost than Navy," *Wall Street Journal*, February 27, 1995.

Roche, James G., and Michael E. Ryan, "Joint Statement of the Honorable James G. Roche Secretary of the Air Force and General Michael E. Ryan, Chief of Staff, United States Air Force," July 11, 2001. As of January 12, 2016: http://lobby.la.psu.edu/_107th/092_C_130_Procurement/Congressional_Hearings/Testimony/H_ArSer_Ryan_071101.htm

Romjue, John L., "The Evolution of the Airland Battle Concept," *Air University Review*, May–June 1984. As of February 22, 2016: http://www.airpower.maxwell.af.mil/airchronicles/aureview/1984/may-jun/romjue.html

Rosen, Stephen Peter, "New Ways of War: Understanding Military Innovation," *International Security*, Vol. 13, No. 1, Summer 1998, pp. 134–168.

Santos, Janie, "Latest 'Vector' Highlights Importance of Discipline," *Air Force News Agency*, September 13, 2007. As of January 25, 2016: http://www.af.mil/News/ArticleDisplay/tabid/223/Article/125741/latest-vector-highlights-importance-of-discipline.aspx

———, "CSAF Releases 'Vector,'" *Defense Media Activity-San Antonio*, July 13, 2010. As of January 25, 2016: http://www.af.mil/News/ArticleDisplay/tabid/223/Article/116162/csaf-releases-vector.aspx

Schriever, Bernard A., "Technology and Aerospace Power in the 1970s," *Air University Review*, September–October 1969. As of February 19, 2016: http://www.airpower.au.af.mil/airchronicles/aureview/1969/sep-oct/schriever.html

Schwartz, Norton A., *CSAF Vector 2010*, July 4, 2010. As of January 25, 2016: http://secure.afa.org/grl/pdfs/CSAFVECTOR2010b.pdf

———, *CSAF Vector 2011*, July 4, 2011. As of January 25, 2016: http://www.airforcemag.com/SiteCollectionDocuments/Reports/2011/July%202011/Day05/CSAF_Vector_2011_070411.pdf

Schwartz, Norton A., and Michael B. Donley, *2008 Air Force Strategic Plan*, Washington, D.C.: Department of the Air Force, October 2008.

Shainin, Jonathan, "Rods from God," *New York Times Magazine*, December 10, 2006. As of January 21, 2016: http://www.nytimes.com/2006/12/10/magazine/10section3a.t-9.html

Shanker, Thom, "2 Top Leaders of Air Force Pushed Out After Inquiry," *New York Times*, June 6, 2008. As of October 27, 2016: http://www.nytimes.com/2008/06/06/washington/05cnd-military.html

Shapley, Deborah, "Space: FAS Redefines the Threat," *Journal of the Federation of American Scientists*, Vol. 57, No. 4, Fall 2004.

Smith, James M., "Air Force Culture and Cohesion: Building an Air and Space Force for the Twenty-First Century," *Airpower Journal*, Fall 1998. As of April 12, 2016: http://www.airpower.maxwell.af.mil/airchronicles/apj/apj98/fal98/smith.html

Smith, Jeffery J., *Tomorrow's Air Force: Tracing the Past, Shaping the Future*, Bloomington, Ind.: Indiana University Press, 2013.

Smith, Perry McCoy, *The Air Force Plans for Peace, 1943–1945*, Baltimore, Md.: Johns Hopkins Press, 1970.

———, "Creating a Strategic Vision: The Value of Long-Range Planning," *Air University Review*, September–October 1986. As of April 20, 2016:
http://www.airpower.maxwell.af.mil/airchronicles/aureview/1986/sep-oct/smith.html

———, "Long-Range Planning: A National Security Necessity," in Perry M. Smith, Jerrold P. Allen, John H. Stewart II, and F. Douglas Whitehouse, eds., *Creating Strategic Vision: Long-Range Planning for National Security*, Washington D.C.: National Defense University Press, 1987. As of April 20, 2016:
http://www.dtic.mil/dtic/tr/fulltext/u2/a187043.pdf

Spiegel, Peter, "Air Force Outlines Strategic Plan: Conventional and Newer Types of Threats Are Both Accounted For," *Los Angeles Times*, February 8, 2008. As of January 13, 2016:
http://articles.latimes.com/2008/feb/08/nation/na-airforce8

Sugden, Bruce M., "Speed Kills: Analyzing the Deployment of Conventional Ballistic Missiles," *International Security*, Vol. 34, No. 1, Summer 2009, p. 113–146.

Sweeney, W. J., L. P. Hammett, A. J. Stosick, and H. S. Tsien, *Aircraft Fuels and Propellants: A Report Prepared for the AAF Scientific Advisory Group*, Vol. 7, Dayton, Ohio: Wright Field, May 1946. As of November 3, 2016:
http://www.governmentattic.org/vonK/AircraftFuelsPropellants_VKarman_V7.pdf

Tebbs, Jeffrey M., "Pruning the Defense Budget," Washington, D.C.: The Brookings Institution, January 2007. As of March 14, 2016:
https://www.brookings.edu/research/pruning-the-defense-budget/

Thomas, Robert McG., Jr., "Col. John Boyd Is Dead at 70; Advanced Air Combat Tactics," *New York Times*, March 13, 1997. As of February 23, 2016:
http://www.nytimes.com/1997/03/13/us/col-john-boyd-is-dead-at-70-advanced-air-combat-tactics.html

Thune, John, "Senator Thune Hails Air Force Report," U.S. Senator for South Dakota John Thune website, January 14, 2008. As of April 11, 2016:
http://www.thune.senate.gov/public/index.cfm/2008/1/press-release-2cea76c5-d975-4bb2-bfcc-8962d40432b9

Tirpak, John A., "The Chief Holds Course," *Air Force Magazine*, January 1998, pp. 37–40.

Thornhill, Paula G., *"Over Not Through": The Search for a Strong, Unified Culture for America's Airmen*, Santa Monica, Calif.: RAND Corporation, OP-386-AF, 2012. As of June 2, 2016:
http://www.rand.org/pubs/occasional_papers/OP386.html

"Transcript on Armed Services Committee Hearing on the Air Force Tanker Competition," U.S. Senator for Alabama Jeff Sessions website, March 5, 2008. As of April 11, 2016:

http://www.sessions.senate.gov/public/index.cfm/news-releases?ID=85c23e85-a3bb-8a86-9ded-2699fc2b38b3

Tsien, H. S., H. L. Dryden, F. L. Wattendorf, F. W. Williams, F. Zwicky, and W. H. Pickering, *Technical Intelligence Supplement: A Report to the AAF Scientific Advisory Group*, Vol. 3, Dayton, Ohio: Wright Field, May 1946. As of November 3, 2016: http://www.governmentattic.org/vonK/TechnicalIntelligenceSupplement_VKarman_V3.pdf

Tsien, H. S., W. R. Sears, Irving L. Ashkenas, C. N. Hasert, and N. M. Newmark, *Aerodynamics and Aircraft Design: A Report of the AAF Scientific Advisory Group*, Vol. 4, Dayton, Ohio: Wright Field, May 1946. As of November 3, 2016: http://www.governmentattic.org/vonK/AerodynamicsAcftDesign_VKarman_V4.pdf

Tyler, Patrick E., "Military Chiefs Detail Plans to Cut Troops, Weapons," *Washington Post*, May 12, 1990, p. A1.

U.S. Air Force, *The 1997 Air Force Long-Range Plan: Summary*, Washington, D.C., 1997.

———, *U.S. Air Force White Paper on Long Range Bombers*, March 1, 1999.
As of November 7, 2016:
https://fas.org/nuke/guide/usa/bomber/bmap99.pdf

———, *America's Air Force Vision 2020: Global Reach, Vigilance, and Power*, 2000.
As of January 26, 2016:
http://webapp1.dlib.indiana.edu/virtual_disk_library/index.cgi/4240529/FID3869/pdfdocs/2020/afvision.pdf

———, *Lasting Heritage . . . Limitless Horizons: A Warfighter's Vision*, February 2006a.
As of February 25, 2016:
http://www.au.af.mil/au/awc/awcgate/af/vision_2025.pdf

———, *Air Force Roadmap 2006–2025*, June 2006b. As of January 22, 2016:
http://www.au.af.mil/au/awc/awcgate/af/af_roadmap_2006-25.pdf

———, "Air Force Chief of Staff Releases Future Roadmap," Washington, D.C., Release No. 040108, January 16, 2008. As of January 22, 2016:
http://www.airforcemag.com/SiteCollectionDocuments/Reports/2008/January/Day17/roadmap011608.pdf

———, "General Norton A. Schwartz," August 2012. As of January 22, 2016:
http://www.af.mil/AboutUs/Biographies/Display/tabid/225/Article/104626/general-norton-a-schwartz.aspx

———, *The World's Greatest Air Force—Powered by Airmen, Fueled by Innovation: A Vision for the United States*, January 2013a.

————, *Global Vigilance, Global Reach, Global Power for America*, 2013b. As of January 25, 2016:
http://www.af.mil/Portals/1/images/airpower/GV_GR_GP_300DPI.pdf

————, "Global Vigilance, Global Reach, Global Power for America," U.S. Air Force YouTube channel, August 22, 2013c. As of January 25, 2016:
https://www.youtube.com/watch?v=ZvWkNGr8RiQ

————, *America's Air Force: A Call to the Future*, July 2014. As November 10, 2016:
http://www.globalsecurity.org/military/library/policy/usaf/usaf-30-year-strategy_2014.pdf

————, *Air Force Future Operating Concept: A View of the Air Force in 2035*, Washington, D.C., September 2015. As of February 26, 2016:
http://www.af.mil/Portals/1/images/airpower/AFFOC.pdf

————, *USAF Strategic Master Plan*, May 2015. As of November 10, 2016:
http://www.af.mil/Portals/1/documents/Force%20Management/Strategic_Master_Plan.pdf

"The U.S. Air Force's New Game Plan in the Asia-Pacific," *The Diplomat,* October 9, 2013. As of January 25, 2016:
http://thediplomat.com/2013/10/the-us-air-forces-new-game-plan-in-the-asia-pacific/

U.S. Department of Defense, "A Commission on Roles and Missions," June 1995, pp. 2–21.

————, "Department of Defense (DoD) Releases Fiscal Year 2017 President's Budget Proposal," Washington, D.C., NR-046-16, February 9, 2016. As of March 14, 2016:
http://www.defense.gov/News/News-Releases/News-Release-View/Article/652687/department-of-defense-dod-releases-fiscal-year-2017-presidents-budget-proposal

U.S. Department of the Navy, *Forward . . . From the Sea*, Washington, D.C., 1992. As of March 14, 2016:
http://www.dtic.mil/jv2010/navy/b014.pdf

U.S. Government Printing Office, *Army Air Forces Field Manual: Employment of Aviation of the Army*, Washington, D.C., FM 1-5, 1943.

Vartabedian, Ralph, "ATF Funding Faces Cut: Defense Firms Plan to Team for Fighter Job," *Los Angeles Times*, July 2, 1986. As of March 9, 2016:
http://articles.latimes.com/1986-07-02/business/fi-387_1_air-force

Vick, Alan, *Proclaiming Airpower: Air Force Narratives and American Public Opinion from 1917 to 2014*, Santa Monica, Calif.: RAND Corporation, RR-1044-AF, 2015. As of October 27, 2016:
http://www.rand.org/pubs/research_reports/RR1044.html

"A View of the Air Force Today," brown paper, Fall 1989.

Von Karman, Theodore, *Toward New Horizons*, Vol. 1., Cameron Station, Alexandria, Va.: Defense Documentation Center for Scientific and Technical Information, 1945. As of November 3, 2016:
http://www.governmentattic.org/vonK/TowardNewHoriz_VKarman_V1.pdf

———, *Where We Stand: A Report Prepared for the AAF Scientific Advisory Group*, Vol. 2, Dayton, Ohio: Wright Field, May 1946. As of November 3, 2016:
http://www.governmentattic.org/vonK/WhereWeStand_VKarman_V2.pdf

Wachter, Chris, "Air-Mindedness: The Core of Successful Air Enterprise Development," *Air and Space Power Journal*, January–February 2012, pp. 1–10. As of January 25, 2016:
http://www.airpower.maxwell.af.mil/digital/pdf/articles/Jan-Feb-2012/Views-Wachter.pdf

War Department Training Regulations, *Air Service: Fundamental Principles for the Employment of the Air Service*, Washington, D.C., TR 440-15, January 26, 1926. As of November 9, 2016:
http://www.au.af.mil/au/awc/awcgate/documents/tr440-15.htm

War Department Field Manual, *Command and Employment of Air Power*, Washington, D.C.: U.S. Government Printing Office, FM 100-20, July 21, 1943. As of February 11, 2016:
http://www.au.af.mil/au/awc/awcgate/documents/fm100-20_jul_1943.pdf

Warden, John A. III, *The Air Campaign: Planning for Combat*, Washington, D.C.: National Defense University Press, 1988. As of February 23, 2016:
http://www.au.af.mil/au/awc/awcgate/warden/warden-all.htm

Walkowicz, T. F., *Toward New Horizons*, Vol. 5, *Future Airborne Armies*, Dayton, Ohio: Wright Field, September 1945. As of November 3, 2016:
http://www.governmentattic.org/vonK/FutureAirborneArmies_VKarman_V5.pdf

Wattendorf, Frank L., H. S. Hsien, and Pol Duwez, *Aircraft Power Plants: A Report to the AAF Scientific Advisory Group*, Vol. 6, Dayton, Ohio: Wright Field, May 1946. As of November 3, 2016:
http://www.governmentattic.org/vonK/AcftPwrPlants_VKarman_V6.pdf

Watts, Barry D., *Long-Range Strike: Imperatives, Urgency and Options*, Washington, D.C.: Center for Strategic and Budgetary Assessments, April 2005. As of January 21, 2016:
http://www.bits.de/NRANEU/docs/R.20050406.LRPS.pdf

Weckerlein, Julie, "Air Force Vision Embraces Warfighters, Heritage," *Air Force Print News*, February 28, 2006. As February 25, 2016:
http://www.af.mil/News/ArticleDisplay/tabid/223/Article/131822/air-force-vision-embraces-warfighters-heritage.aspx

Weissert, Carol S., "Policy Entrepreneurs, Policy Opportunists and Legislative Effectiveness," *American Political Quarterly*, Vol. 19, No. 2, April 1991, pp. 262–274.

Welsh, Mark A. III, "The Strategic Choices and Management Review," Washington, D.C.: Department of the Air Force Presentation to the House Armed Services Committee, September 18, 2013. As of April 11, 2016: http://docs.house.gov/meetings/AS/AS00/20130918/101291/HHRG-113-AS00-Wstate-WelshIIIUSAFM-20130918.pdf

Widnall, Sheila E., and Ronald R. Fogleman, *Global Presence*, Washington, D.C.: National Defense University, Institute for National Strategic Studies, Fort Lesley J. McNair, 1995.

Wong, Kristina, "Pentagon Welcomes Budget Deal but Wants More Money," *Washington Times*, December 11, 2013. As of April 11, 2016: http://www.washingtontimes.com/news/2013/dec/11/pentagon-welcomes-budget-deal-but-more-defense-spe

Worden, Michael, *Rise of the Fighter Generals. The Problem of Air Force Leadership 1945–1982*, Maxwell Air Force Base, Ala.: Air University Press, March 1998. As of July 11, 2016: http://www.dtic.mil/cgi-bin/GetTRDoc?AD=ADA338755

Y'Blood, William T., "Metamorphosis: The Air Force Approaches the Next Century," in Bernard C. Nalty, ed., *Winged Sword, Winged Shield: A History of the United States Air Force 1950–1997*, Vol. II, Washington, D.C.: Air Force History and Museums Program, 1997.